The
Mansion
on
Turtle Creek
Cookbook

The Mansion on Turtle Creek Cookbook

by
Dean Fearing

edited by Dotty Griffith

Weidenfeld & Nicolson
New York

Published by Weidenfeld & Nicolson, New York
A Division of Wheatland Corporation
10 East 53rd Street
New York, NY 10022

Published in Canada by General Publishing Company, Ltd.

Library of Congress Cataloging-in-Publication Data

Fearing, Dean.
  The Mansion on Turtle Creek cookbook.

  Includes index.
  1. Cookery, American—Southwestern style.
2. Mansion on Turtle Creek (Hotel: Dallas, Tex.)
I. Griffith, Dotty.   II. Mansion on Turtle Creek
(Hotel: Dallas, Tex.)   III. Title.
TX715.F288   1987   641.5'09764'2812   87-21535
ISBN 1-55584-176-7

Manufactured in the United States of America
Designed by Irving Perkins Associates
First Edition
10   9   8   7   6   5   4   3   2   1

The photographs of the restaurant entrance, the veranda, and the bar were taken by Jaime Ardilles Arce.

All other photography by Ben Marshall, John Wong, and Barth Tillotson, Greg Booth + Associates/Dallas.

THIS BOOK IS DEDICATED TO
THE NEW GENERATION OF AMERICAN CHEFS WHOSE
VISION AND SPIRIT ARE TAKING AMERICAN
CUISINE TO ITS DESERVED HEIGHTS.

Acknowledgments

My very special thanks to the people who made this a living cookbook . . .

Robert Zimmer, who had the keen sense to recognize, on behalf of Rosewood Hotels, Inc., the incomparable potential of The Mansion on Turtle Creek. His vision of excellence, style, and grace has enabled me to pursue my own culinary vision.

Patrick Willis, for support and direction I cannot even begin to describe and for being with me through both the pleasant and unpleasant junctions of this book.

Robert Sheldon Reash, Jr., executive sous chef, whose considerable talent kept the magic alive in The Mansion on Turtle Creek kitchen while I was working on this project.

Robert Zielinski, our pastry chef, and Ruth Sobel-Anderson for devoting time in their schedules to help us re-create the most wonderful course at the end of the meal for the book.

To each and every one on my kitchen staff for believing in the common sense of good cooking. They all know that I couldn't have done this without their unfailing good humor. I hope they carry The Mansion on Turtle Creek tradition with them wherever they go.

Bill Shoaf, for his overall assistance and superb ability to ensure that food and wine make a perfect marriage.

Dotty Griffith, for her talent, support, and understanding. Her endless hours of typing and retyping as she deciphered my favorite recipes made this cookbook possible.

Kyra Effren, for testing each recipe. Her understanding and enthusiasm made a very tedious job fun and exciting.

Wolfgang Puck, for his inspiration, friendship, and encouragement.

Lauren McGuire, for her devoted assistance at all times with any need and for keeping my calendar up-to-date!

Jean-Pierre Albertinetti, maître d', and the entire dining room staff for always enthusiastically endorsing our kitchen.

Peter Rosenberg, executive chef at The Hotel Bel-Air, for his support and contributions in the early stages of the book.

My Neiman-Marcus InCircle friends, for their support and participation in tasting and testing the recipes.

Jan Miller and Mary Homi, who diligently and tirelessly sought to bring together the talents of many creative people.

Michael Polito, whose artistry brought the exquisite beauty of ZEN Floral Studio alive in the restaurant and in the photographs throughout the book. He has been an inspiration to us all.

Barth Tillotson, Ben Marshall, and John Wong of Greg Booth + Associates of Dallas, for their inspired production of our photography.

Sharon Hammond and Eileen Houser for their support at the start of this project.

The many vintners who helped me understand that there is the same loving care in the fields as in the kitchen.

Judie Choate, for professional assistance, talent, and enthusiasm in bringing the entire project together at the final hour.

My parents, Tom and Ollie, without whose support of my endless culinary journeys I might never have traveled this road.

Our guests and valued friends, for the trust and enthusiastic support of our menus as we have endeavored to create culinary legends.

A SPECIAL TRIBUTE to Caroline Rose Hunt for making the achievement of so many dreams possible.

Contents

THE MANSION ON TURTLE CREEK STYLE
Robert Zimmer
xi

THE MANSION ON TURTLE CREEK CUISINE
Dean Fearing
xiii

The Mansion on Turtle Creek embodies what I believe to be Rosewood's total commitment to excellence—from the immaculately appointed private residences to the restaurant's unsurpassed cuisine. It is small and luxurious in the European tradition yet totally American in style and ambiance. The Mansion on Turtle Creek provides what I believe to be unparalleled service in a compound of life and environment in balance. It is my most meaningful accomplishment that in establishing an oasis that transcends time, we present to our guests a deep sense of well-being and belonging with the warm welcome extended to dear friends.

It is not coincidental that our restaurant has the comforting look and feel of a gracious home. Indeed, The Mansion on Turtle Creek was constructed as a private dwelling for cotton magnate Sheppard King in 1925. This Italian Renaissance landmark has changed hands throughout the years but fortunately always to those who appreciated its beauty. The rich Italian tiles, pink marble, carved fireplaces, stained glass windows, and inlaid wooden ceilings are still an integral part of the design of The Mansion on Turtle Creek.

Rosewood Hotels acquired this historic residence in 1979. With its preservation the paramount issue, this masterpiece was lovingly restored to its proper place in Dallas's heritage as Rosewood's flagship hotel and restaurant. Upon opening, The Mansion on Turtle Creek received international acclaim, highlighted by the prestigious Keystone Award given in 1981 by the Historic Preservation League of Dallas.

An emphasis on the creation of a lifestyle has challenged the entire staff. Attentiveness to every detail, to every comfort, a standard of grace, manner, and style, is paramount throughout The Mansion on Turtle Creek. This attention is nowhere more apparent than in our famous cuisine. For the food, imaginatively and inspiringly presented, is exemplary of Rosewood's philosophy of expressing a concept of excellence.

We present food that abounds with a fullness of imagination. Our triumphant combinations of the freshest seasonal fare do not pretend to imitate French, Italian, or Oriental cuisines, but proudly reflect an American and regional idiom. This native American cuisine appears in a newer, lighter mode, yet it demands the same intricate balance of flavors and respect for fine ingredients of more traditional fare. Its signature characteristic, however, is its devotion to the colorful and unconventional combinations of our native Southwest foods.

The Mansion on Turtle Creek Cookbook has been conceived as a means to help you re-create The Mansion on Turtle Creek experience in your own home. In addition to Chef Fearing's exciting and innovative recipes, we present the combinations of food and wine—with attention to texture, color, taste, and style—that reflect our fervent belief that a fine meal is not merely a recipe.

We have taken every care to create a cookbook that will transcend time in the same manner as The Mansion on Turtle Creek. These pages, under the hand of a master chef and connoisseur of fine food, present the ambiance and flavor savored daily at The Mansion on Turtle Creek: a keen sense of friendship, hospitality, and family. Just as our guests visit The Mansion on Turtle Creek time and again, we know you will often come back to these pages for gracious dining.

Robert Zimmer
President
Rosewood Hotels, Inc.

The Mansion on Turtle Creek Cuisine

Several years ago, "talking food" after a long day in the kitchen, someone asked why we couldn't try what chefs in California and New York were doing—using local products to produce regional or American cuisine. I had always used "the best" and "the freshest," but I had overlooked the *very* best and the *very* freshest right at my door—products produced for local cooking needs or found in the local hunting preserves. I began to experiment using ingredients that Dallas diners had never encountered outside Tex-Mex restaurants: chili peppers, jicama, native herbs, tomatillos, cilantro, avocado, chayote squash, papaya, and mango. I included the local wild game, birds and venison never seen in our fine restaurants, and used grilling and smoking techniques that were identified more with cowboys and chuckwagons than with a 5-star restaurant's kitchen. And so evolved Southwest cuisine and the unique dining experience we now offer at The Mansion on Turtle Creek.

The philosophy of The Mansion on Turtle Creek is to reflect a Southwest identity throughout the hotel. This commitment has allowed me to create a menu using products indigenous to the region based on its ethnic foods and tastes. The result is a singular refinement of older cuisines: bold in flavor, sophisticated in presentation, and, though sometimes unpredictable, always, I think, offering exciting dining at The Mansion on Turtle Creek.

When deciding whether a certain dish or menu is right for The Mansion on Turtle Creek, I examine its barest essence—the ingredients and flavors—and apply common-sense judgment about good cooking. Does it taste good? And can it be prepared beautifully? If the answer to each question is an enthusiastic "yes," then it will appear in the dining room. I rely on my palate above all, and then my eye, to prepare food that signifies the level of quality The Mansion on Turtle Creek represents and that will offer a true taste of the Southwest.

What is Southwest cuisine? To me, it incorporates products native to the Southwest in recipes prepared and presented using nontraditional methods. Although the techniques I use are often classic in the culinary sense, the flavor combinations are quite new. The true test for this cuisine is taste; the food must have backbone and soul. If it is bland, it does not accurately represent the zest and earthiness of the region. Like other regional cuisines being practiced today, Southwest cuisine is a refinement of our locale's traditional folk styles.

For me, there are other influences as well, including my own southern upbringing and my enthusiasm for the foods and flavors of the Orient. I was also trained to be a chef de cuisine in the classic French fashion. The fine sauces and superb preparation techniques are ingrained into my cooking sense. All of these have combined to assist me in putting my own stamp on the Southwest. The examples are found in the recipes themselves.

A dish that exemplifies these principles is the Lobster Taco. Hardly southwestern in origin, lobster nevertheless takes to the flavors of the Southwest when it is rolled in a perfectly fresh flour tortilla, sauced with Yellow Tomato Salsa, and garnished with Jicama Salad. When I first proposed to offer it as a daily special, we wondered whether an everyday food like tacos could be served in a fine restaurant, but we all agreed to give it a try. Patrons immediately loved it, and it has, in fact, become a signature dish at The Mansion on Turtle Creek. And once you've tried a Lobster Taco, you'll know it is not "everyday" food.

Some of the recipes may seem very long and involved. That is because the entrées often do not require an accompaniment. Our garnishes are actually "side dishes." Once you've completed the recipe, from main component to sauce to garnish, you have a meal! To achieve the desired results in appearance and cooking technique, you should be comfortable with the foods and techniques described in the chapter called "Dean Fearing's Southwest Kitchen." Simply chopping peppers won't give the "confetti" look that characterizes my salsas and relishes. Techniques for grilling and smoking are very different from the traditional, and the objectives in smoking meats and vegetables are my own. Smoking meat and poultry is usually a cooking process, whereas smoking vegetables is done primarily for flavoring. Using chilies creatively requires discipline and skill since it is not necessarily the heat but the flavor you want to achieve. Their natural flavor must blend with the other flavors in the recipe to produce a perfect marriage of tastes.

The wine suggestions throughout the book will assist you in presenting the total meal. Each wine recommended is our personal choice from our extensive, award-winning wine cellar. You can substitute your own favorite as long as it is of the same type—American vineyards being our first choice! All of these tips will help you create The Mansion on Turtle Creek menus in your kitchen.

Using indigenous ingredients in a particular style is not enough to create a unique cuisine. Recently, I've turned my attention not only to the historical origin of the ingredients but to the sources from which we obtain them.

Our standards are high. We use only the finest quality and uncompromisingly fresh products. Our concern (and our patrons' concern) for nutrition and the wholesome integrity of food has led us to develop as many local sources as possible. Only in that way can we be assured of absolute freshness. We have growers in West Texas who produce quail to our specifications and ship them fresh whenever we need them. Others grow and process game birds such as chukar and pheasant. Farmers in Decatur, north of Dallas, grow raspberries for us; in East Texas, growers produce blueberries. Other farmers found in different areas all over the state grow peaches; vine-ripened yellow and red tomatoes; all varieties of corn, from baby to sweet; lettuces of every shade and variety; peppers of myriad colors, sizes, and hotness levels; and herbs, particularly the Mexican ones such as epazote and mint marigold.

We obtain wild game to order from a game cooperative, Broken Arrow Ranch, run by my good friend Mike Hughes, in tiny Ingram, Texas, in the Texas Hill Country. Even cheeses are produced especially for us. Another friend, Paula Lambert of the Dallas Mozzarella Company, was one of the first local suppliers of custom-made products for The Mansion on Turtle Creek. Her efforts began a trend that is expanding and that, I believe, will be the way of the future. You will find some of these as well as other sources of Southwest products listed in the back of the book so that you can be assured of authenticity in reproducing my recipes.

I am of a new generation of American chefs who find stimulation in sharing ideas with and learning from chefs and cooks from my own and other cultures and in talking with those who know and care about food, then incorporating what I've learned into my own personal style of cuisine. When I first began to develop The Mansion on Turtle Creek's Southwest "regional" menu, colleagues kept telling me to be a little more cautious in my approach—"the restaurant guests aren't ready to experience a new cuisine." A dedicated staff and adventuresome guests, working together, have proved skeptics wrong. We have incorporated the foods of the earth from the Plains Indians, the foods of the soul from the northern Mexicans, and the foods of substance from the American cowboys into our very own Southwest cuisine.

This is a cook's book! Use it! Don't put it on the coffee table. Put it in the kitchen and have fun re-creating the dining experience we offer, daily, at The Mansion on Turtle Creek: a taste of the American Southwest.

Dean Fearing
September 1987

Four views of The Mansion on Turtle Creek: the entrance (preceding page); the veranda (left); the bar (below); and the main dining room (right).

Dean Fearing with Paula
Lambert, owner of the
Mozzarella Company.

At Broken Arrow Ranch with Mike Hughes (left),
owner of the ranch, and his associate Perrin Wells
(right).

With Robert Zimmer (left),
president of Rosewood Hotels,
Inc., and Jean-Pierre Albertinetti
(right), maître d' of The Mansion
on Turtle Creek dining room.

At American Food Service, with Joey La
Barba (left) and Lucian La Barba (center),
the owners.

Starters

Appetizers

WARM LOBSTER TACO WITH YELLOW TOMATO SALSA
AND JICAMA SALAD

STIR-FRIED SMOKED SHRIMP WITH SPICY PEANUT SAUCE
AND PINEAPPLE CHUTNEY

PAN-FRIED LOUISIANA CRABCAKES
WITH SMOKED BELL PEPPER BUTTER SAUCE

FRIED OYSTERS STUFFED WITH CRABMEAT
WITH CAJUN TARTAR SAUCE

GRILLED JOHN DORY WITH CRUSHED MUSTARD SEEDS
AND TOMATO COULIS

SMOKED CRISP SWEETBREADS ON BREADED EGGPLANT ROUNDS
WITH YELLOW TOMATO-BASIL SAUCE

PAN-FRIED BREADED CLAMS WITH GREEN ONION PASTA
AND ROASTED GARLIC SAUCE

SMOKED RAINBOW TROUT WITH SORREL
AND GRILLED TOMATO SAUCE

WILD DUCK PÂTÉ WITH PICKLED OKRA

WARM LOBSTER TACO WITH YELLOW TOMATO SALSA AND JICAMA SALAD

*Serves
6*

I created this dish in early 1986 and it quickly became my signature appetizer on The Mansion on Turtle Creek menu. The name "Lobster Taco" perfectly illustrates the casual elegance that characterizes Southwest cuisine. Its appeal is rooted in the combination of rich lobster and a simple flour tortilla. The salsa and salad garnishes produce an explosion of color that promises exciting dining.

4 *1-pound lobsters*
6 *7-inch fresh Flour Tortillas*
3 *tablespoons corn oil*
1 *cup grated jalapeño Jack cheese*

1 *cup shredded spinach leaves*
  Yellow Tomato Salsa
  Jicama Salad

Preheat oven to 300°. Fill a large stock pot with lightly salted water and bring to a boil over high heat. Add lobsters and cook for about 8 minutes or until just done. Drain and let lobsters cool slightly. Wrap tortillas tightly in foil and place in preheated 300° oven for about 15 minutes or until heated through. Keep warm until ready to use.

Remove meat from lobster tails being careful not to tear it apart. Cut meat into thin medallions (or medium-sized dice, if meat breaks apart).

Heat oil in a medium sauté pan over medium heat and sauté lobster medallions until just heated through.

Spoon equal portions of warm lobster medallions into the center of each warm tortilla. Sprinkle with equal portions of grated cheese and shredded spinach.

Roll tortillas into a cylinder shape and place each one on a warm serving plate with the edge facing the bottom.

Surround the taco with Yellow Tomato Salsa and garnish each side with a small mound of Jicama Salad.

FLOUR TORTILLAS

2 cups sifted all-purpose flour
1 teaspoon baking powder
1/2 teaspoon salt

1/2 teaspoon sugar
1 tablespoon vegetable shortening
1/2 cup warm water, approximately

Sift together flour, baking powder, salt, and sugar. Cut in shortening until flour looks as though it has small peas in it. Add enough warm water to make a soft dough. Mix well and knead on a well-floured board for 3 to 5 minutes or until shiny and elastic. Cover dough and let rest for 30 minutes, out of draft.

Form dough into balls about 2 to 2½ inches in diameter. On a lightly floured board, roll into circles about 7 inches in diameter and ¼ inch thick.

Cook on a hot, ungreased griddle for about 2 minutes or until lightly browned on the edges. Turn and cook on the other side for about 1 minute or until edges are brown. Keep warm, tightly wrapped in foil if serving right away, or reheat, tightly wrapped in foil, at 300° for about 10 to 15 minutes or until heated through.

Makes 10 to 12 tortillas.

YELLOW TOMATO SALSA

2 pints yellow cherry tomatoes or 1
   pound yellow tomatoes
1 large shallot, very finely minced
1 large clove garlic, very finely
   minced
2 tablespoons finely minced fresh
   cilantro
1 tablespoon champagne vinegar or
   white wine vinegar

2 serrano chilies, seeded and
   minced
2 teaspoons lime juice
   Salt to taste
1 tablespoon maple syrup (use only
   if tomatoes are not sweet enough)

In a food processor, using the steel blade, process tomatoes until well chopped. Do not purée. Combine tomatoes and their juices with shallot, garlic, cilantro, vinegar, chilies, lime juice, and salt, mixing well. Add maple syrup, if needed, to balance flavor and sweeten slightly.

Cover and refrigerate for at least 2 hours or until very cold.

NOTE: For a crunchier, more typical salsa, put tomatoes through fine die of a food grinder.

JICAMA SALAD

½ small jicama, peeled and cut into fine julienne strips

½ small red bell pepper, seeds and membranes removed, cut into fine julienne strips

½ small yellow bell pepper, seeds and membranes removed, cut into fine julienne strips

½ small zucchini (only part that has green skin attached), cut into fine julienne strips

½ small carrot, peeled and cut into fine julienne strips

4 tablespoons cold-pressed peanut oil

2 tablespoons lime juice

Salt to taste

Cayenne pepper to taste

Combine vegetables, oil, lime juice, salt, and cayenne to taste and toss to mix well.

Advance Preparations:

1. Lobsters may be boiled up to a day ahead. Remove tail meat and slice. Store, covered and refrigerated.
2. Yellow Tomato Salsa must be prepared at least 2 hours (but no more than 8 hours) ahead and refrigerated, covered, until cold. Adjust seasoning.
3. Jicama Salad may be prepared several hours ahead and refrigerated. In that case, omit salt until almost ready to serve.
4. Cheese and spinach for tacos may be shredded several hours ahead. Wrap tightly and refrigerate.

 WINE SUGGESTION:

SAUVIGNON BLANC, ARBOR CREST, 1985
Dry, medium-bodied wine with lemon-lime overtones in the nose and a crisp, melon citrus taste to enhance the lobster and its tart salsa.

Stir-Fried Smoked Shrimp with Spicy Peanut Sauce and Pineapple Chutney

*Serves
6*

This was the first recipe in which I used cold smoke just to flavor, not to cook. The shrimp is flavored over cold smoke, then stir-fried just before serving. The dish also represents a combination of Oriental and Southwest flavors and cooking techniques.

24 medium-sized Gulf shrimp (16 to 20 per pound), peeled and deveined, tails intact
4 tablespoons sesame oil

Salt to taste
Spicy Peanut Sauce
Pineapple Chutney
¹/₄ cup 1-inch pieces of chives

Place shrimp in a covered smoker using the technique for flavoring (see page 272). Smoke for 5 to 8 minutes, just to take on smoke flavor. Shrimp should be raw when removed from the smoker.

Heat 2 tablespoons sesame oil in a large sauté pan over high heat. Season shrimp with salt to taste. Place 12 shrimp in the oil and stir-fry for 3 to 4 minutes or until shrimp are no longer transparent.

Remove from sauté pan and keep warm.

Add remaining oil to pan, season remaining shrimp, and stir-fry as above. Keep warm.

Ladle Spicy Peanut Sauce onto six warm serving plates, using just enough to make a thin layer over the entire surface.

Place a small mound of Pineapple Chutney in the center of each plate. Arrange 4 stir-fried shrimp on each plate with tails toward chutney.

Sprinkle chutney with chopped chives and serve immediately.

SPICY PEANUT SAUCE

1 cup raw peanuts, shelled
1/2 cup sweet rice wine vinegar
1/4 cup plum wine
1/4 cup mirin (Japanese sweet rice
  wine)
2 tablespoons soy sauce
2 tablespoons balsamic vinegar
2 tablespoons chopped green onions
  Leaves from 3 sprigs fresh
  cilantro, chopped
2 cloves garlic, chopped

2 shallots, chopped
2 tablespoons grated fresh ginger,
  with juice
3 serrano chilies, seeded and
  chopped
1/2 cup brown veal demi-glace (see
  page 263)
1 cup chicken stock (see page 262)
1 cup heavy cream
  Lime juice to taste
  Salt to taste

Preheat oven to 350°. Rub skins off peanuts and place on a roasting pan. Roast peanuts in preheated 350° oven for 8 minutes or until light brown.

Place roasted peanuts, rice wine vinegar, plum wine, mirin, soy sauce, balsamic vinegar, green onions, cilantro, garlic, shallots, ginger, and chilies in a medium saucepan over medium-high heat. Cook, stirring frequently, for about 8 minutes or until almost all the liquid has evaporated and the remainder is thick and syrupy but not caramelized or burned.

Stir demi-glace and chicken stock into saucepan. Cook for about 8 minutes or until liquid is reduced by half. Add cream and bring to a boil. Remove from heat and pour into a blender. Blend for about 4 minutes or until very smooth. Strain through a fine sieve.

Season to taste with lime juice and salt. Keep warm.

PINEAPPLE CHUTNEY

³/₄ cup fresh orange juice
*¹/₄ cup passion fruit purée or juice (if
   unavailable, use an additional ¹/₄
   cup orange juice)*
*1 green onion, cleaned, trimmed,
   and chopped*
1 shallot, chopped
1 clove garlic, chopped
*1 jalapeño chili, seeded and
   chopped*
*1 tablespoon grated fresh ginger,
   with juice*

1 teaspoon chili powder
1 teaspoon curry powder
*¹/₂ ripe fresh pineapple, peeled, cored,
   and cut into small cubes*
*¹/₂ tablespoon finely chopped fresh
   mint*
*¹/₂ tablespoon finely chopped fresh
   basil*
*¹/₄ red bell pepper, seeded and cut
   into julienne strips*

Place orange juice, passion fruit purée, green onion, shallot, garlic, jalapeño, ginger, chili powder, and curry powder in a medium saucepan and cook over medium-high heat for approximately 10 minutes. Bring to a boil and cook, stirring frequently, until liquid is reduced to ¹/₄ cup.

Remove saucepan from heat and strain liquid into a medium bowl. Add pineapple, mint, basil, and red bell pepper; mix well. Cool slightly, cover, and refrigerate several hours to chill before serving.

Advance Preparation:
1. Pineapple Chutney may be prepared up to 3 days in advance. Cover tightly and refrigerate.
2. Spicy Peanut Sauce may be prepared several hours ahead; keep warm. Reheat gently if necessary.
3. If desired, smoke shrimp early in the day and refrigerate. Stir-fry just before serving.

 WINE SUGGESTION:

CHARDONNAY, WILLIAM WHEELER, 1984
A medium-bodied dry wine with a smoky honey nose and full flavors of pear and pineapple to complement the blends of smoke, nut, and fruit with the shrimp.

PAN-FRIED LOUISIANA CRABCAKES
WITH SMOKED BELL PEPPER BUTTER SAUCE

*Serves
4*

This is one of the most popular appetizers at The Mansion on Turtle Creek. It is based on a traditional southern recipe to which I've added a tantalizing Southwest flavor by using cold smoked bell pepper in the sauce. People are intrigued by the subtle smoky flavor, and its source is a frequent subject of inquiry.

1 extra large egg, beaten
1 tablespoon mayonnaise
   Salt to taste
1/4 teaspoon ground black pepper
1/4 teaspoon curry powder
3 or 4 drops Tabasco sauce
1 teaspoon Worcestershire sauce
1 tablespoon lemon juice
1/8 teaspoon ground cloves
1/8 teaspoon cayenne pepper
1/2 teaspoon paprika
1/4 teaspoon dry mustard

1/4 teaspoon celery salt
1 pound fresh jumbo lump
   crabmeat, all shell removed
3 to 4 tablespoons dry bread
   crumbs
2 cups corn or peanut oil,
   approximately
   Smoked Bell Pepper Butter Sauce
12 3- to 4-inch pieces of chives
24 pieces of Spicy Fried Pasta,
   approximately 5 to 6 inches long

Combine egg, mayonnaise, and seasonings. Add crabmeat and enough bread crumbs to absorb excess moisture.

Stir to blend well. Mixture should be firm enough to hold together. Adjust seasoning as desired. Form crabmeat mixture into 8 patties. Place on wax paper for about 20 minutes to dry slightly. Pour oil into a skillet to a depth of 1/2 inch and heat to 350°.

Fry crabcakes for about 3 to 4 minutes per side or until golden brown on both sides. Do not crowd pan. Fry in several batches, if necessary. Drain on paper towel.

Ladle Smoked Bell Pepper Butter

Sauce onto four warm serving plates, using enough to cover the entire surface.

In the center of each plate, place 2 crabcakes. Fan 3 strips of chives and 6 strips of Spicy Fried Pasta next to crabcakes and serve immediately.

SMOKED BELL PEPPER BUTTER SAUCE

1/4 red bell pepper
1/4 yellow bell pepper
1/4 poblano chili
2 cups cold, unsalted butter cut into
 tablespoons
1/2 cup sliced fresh mushrooms
2 small shallots, diced

1 sprig fresh thyme
1/4 cup white wine
1/4 cup white wine vinegar
1/2 cup chicken stock (see page 262)
1/4 cup heavy cream
 Salt to taste
 Lemon juice to taste

Smoke bell peppers and poblano chili for about 20 minutes or until peppers and chili have taken on smoke flavor (see page 272).

Peel peppers and chili. Seed, remove membranes, and cut into small dice (see page 271). Reserve.

Heat 1 tablespoon butter in a medium saucepan over medium heat. Sauté mushrooms, shallots, and thyme for 2 minutes. Add wine, vinegar, and stock and cook for about 10 minutes or until liquid is reduced by half. Add cream and cook an additional 5 minutes or until liquid is reduced by half.

Off heat, whisk in remaining butter piece by piece. Strain. Season to taste with salt and lemon juice. Fold in diced peppers and chili. Keep warm until ready to use.

SPICY FRIED PASTA

2 tablespoons tomato paste
1/2 tablespoon chili powder
1/2 tablespoon cayenne pepper; use
 more for intense heat
1 1/2 tablespoons minced jalapeño
 chili, seeds removed

1/2 teaspoon salt
1 extra large egg yolk
1 teaspoon peanut oil
1/4 to 1/2 cup water
2 cups semolina flour
2 to 3 cups vegetable oil

Combine tomato paste, chili powder, cayenne pepper, jalapeño, and salt in a blender or food processor. Blend until smooth.

Mix egg yolk, peanut oil, and water. Pour into food processor bowl. Add flour and blend to make pasta dough according to pasta machine manufacturer's directions. Run through pasta machine and extrude for very thin noodles.

Heat vegetable oil to 350° in a deep sauté pan. Deep-fry small amounts of pasta dough cut into 6-inch strips for about 45 seconds or just until crisp. Do not allow pasta to curl or to darken or turn brown. It should remain straight and bright red.

Advance Preparation:
1. Sauce may be prepared several hours in advance but must be kept warm.
2. Crabcakes may be made several hours ahead and refrigerated. Fry just before serving.

 WINE SUGGESTION:

FUMÉ BLANC, DRY CREEK, 1985
Medium-bodied with a grassy nose, fresh, structured fruit flavors, and crisp finish, this wine can stand up to the spice of the crab and the richness of the sauce.

FRIED OYSTERS STUFFED WITH CRABMEAT
WITH CAJUN TARTAR SAUCE

*Serves
4*

When I visited my friend Larry Forgione in his New York restaurant An American Place, he introduced me to this method of frying oysters in the half-shell. I was intrigued and immediately returned to my kitchen at The Mansion on Turtle Creek to create this appetizer with a Cajun accent.

16 oysters in shells
   Seaweed for garnish, if available
   (1 large bunch cilantro, washed
   and trimmed, may be
   substituted)
 1 extra large egg, beaten
 2 tablespoons mayonnaise
 2 tablespoons heavy cream
1/4 teaspoon ground black pepper
1/4 teaspoon curry powder
 3 or 4 drops Tabasco sauce
 1 teaspoon Worcestershire sauce

 1 tablespoon lemon juice
1/8 teaspoon ground cloves
1/8 teaspoon cayenne pepper
1/2 teaspoon paprika
1/4 teaspoon dry mustard
1/4 teaspoon celery seed
   Salt to taste
1/2 pound jumbo lump crabmeat, all
   shell removed
 1 cup very fine bread crumbs
 8 cups peanut oil
   Cajun Tartar Sauce

Scrub oyster shells and open, reserving 1 tablespoon oyster liquor for tartar sauce (or have fishmonger do this). Leave oysters in half-shells but sever the muscle that fastens to shell. Reserve 4 oyster shells for garnish.

If seaweed is available, rinse well, then blanch in boiling water for 1 minute. Drain and submerge in ice water. Drain and pat dry; reserve for garnish.

Combine egg, mayonnaise, cream, and seasonings. Fold in crabmeat. Add 1 to 2 tablespoons bread crumbs, mixing well.

Adjust seasonings to taste. Mixture should not be too stiff to spread or too wet to adhere. Add more bread crumbs if necessary.

Spread crab mixture over oysters on the half-shell. Make certain each oyster is covered completely and the edges are sealed. Sprinkle each oyster with a heavy coat of the remaining bread crumbs. Set aside on wax paper and allow to dry for 30 minutes.

In a small deep fryer, heat oil to 350°.

When hot, carefully submerge the whole oysters (including shells) in oil. Do not crowd. (You may want to test one oyster before proceeding. If crabmeat mixture starts to fall apart in oil, the mixture is too wet. Add more bread crumbs.)

Fry oysters for about 2½ minutes or until golden brown. Remove from oil and drain on paper towel. Keep hot.

Spread seaweed over the surface of four room-temperature serving plates. Place 4 fried oysters stuffed with crabmeat on each plate at the 12, 3, 6, and 9 o'clock positions. In the middle of each plate, center an oyster shell filled with Cajun Tartar Sauce.

Serve immediately. Pass extra sauce, if desired.

CAJUN TARTAR SAUCE

1 cup mayonnaise
2 tablespoons Creole mustard
2 tablespoons thin-sliced green portion of green onions
2 teaspoons chopped, drained capers
1 tablespoon reserved oyster liquor
2 teaspoons Worcestershire sauce

1 teaspoon Tabasco sauce
1 teaspoon lemon juice
1 teaspoon finely grated fresh horseradish
1 clove garlic, finely chopped
  Salt to taste
  Ground black pepper to taste

Combine all ingredients. Mix well to blend. Spoon some sauce into each of 4 reserved oyster shells.

Reserve remaining sauce to pass at the table.

Advance Preparation:
1. You may scrub oysters, open shells, reserve, and strain oyster liquor several hours ahead. Keep refrigerated until ready to use.
2. Seaweed garnish may be blanched and refrigerated up to 1 day ahead.
3. Sauce may be prepared several hours ahead and kept cool until ready to serve.

 WINE SUGGESTION:

CHARDONNAY, CAKEBREAD CELLARS, 1985
A medium-bodied wine with some spice and oak in nose and lean, lemony fruit flavors that will balance the richness of oysters and sauce.

GRILLED JOHN DORY WITH CRUSHED MUSTARD SEEDS AND TOMATO COULIS

Serves 6

This recipe was given to me by Wolfgang Puck. Well known for his innovative California cuisine, Wolfgang has been a guiding force for me through my early years of chefhood. He doesn't understand why I don't change my last name to "Garcia, the Southwest chef."

6 6-ounce John Dory fillets (fillet of lemon sole or any flaky, white fish may be substituted)
2 tablespoons olive oil
   Salt to taste

Ground black pepper to taste
3 tablespoons Pommery mustard
   Tomato Coulis
6 sprigs fresh thyme or tarragon for garnish

Preheat oven to 400°. Preheat grill or light coals.

Make sure grates are clean, and lightly rub or brush with vegetable oil before placing fish on grill. Brush fillets with 2 tablespoons olive oil and season to taste with salt and pepper.

Place on hot grill for 1 to 2 minutes just to mark one side. Turn fillets and place in a baking pan large enough to hold all fillets in one layer.

Brush cooked side with mustard and bake in preheated 400° oven for 5 minutes or until fish flakes. Allow 5 minutes total cooking time for each ½ inch of thickness at thickest part. Do not overcook. Fish should be moist.

Ladle Tomato Coulis onto six warm serving plates, using just enough to make a thin layer over the entire surface.

Place a fillet in the center of each plate and garnish top with a sprig of fresh thyme or tarragon. Serve immediately.

NOTE: If grill is not available, fillets may be cooked first in a sauté pan and then in the oven. To do so, heat 2 to 3 tablespoons olive oil in a sauté pan over high heat. Season fillets to taste with salt and pepper. Cook on one side for about 2 to 3 minutes or until fillets are light golden at edges. Brush cooked side with mustard and place in oven as above.

TOMATO COULIS

2 medium tomatoes
2 shallots, minced
1 cup white wine
½ cup fish stock (see page 265)
1 cup heavy cream

1 cup very cold unsalted butter, cut
   into small pieces
   Cayenne pepper to taste
   Salt to taste
   Ground black pepper to taste

Peel and seed tomatoes. In a food processor, using the steel blade, purée to a fine, even consistency. Set aside.

Combine shallots, wine, and fish stock in a medium saucepan. Bring to a boil over medium heat; reduce heat and simmer for about 10 minutes or until reduced to ½ cup.

Stir in cream and again bring liquid to a boil. Cook for about 5 minutes or until sauce has thickened.

Whisk in butter one piece at a time until well blended. Season to taste with cayenne, salt, and pepper; strain through a sieve. Gently fold in tomatoes. Keep warm until ready to use.

Advance Preparation:
1. Coulis may be made several hours in advance but must be kept warm. If reheating is necessary, briefly do so over very low heat so sauce does not break.

 WINE SUGGESTION:

CABERNET BLANC, STERLING, 1985
Dry rosé wine with slight berry nose and a tart fruit taste provides the softness to complement the fish and a complexity needed for the sauce.

SMOKED CRISP SWEETBREADS ON BREADED EGGPLANT ROUNDS WITH YELLOW TOMATO-BASIL SAUCE

*Serves
4*

Sweetbreads represent a culinary quest—an attempt to win a badge of honor. For some reason, almost all chefs feel compelled to try to make diners want to order them. This is my best effort.

1 to 1¼ pounds (1 large pair or 2
  small pairs) veal sweetbreads
¼ teaspoon salt
  Juice of 2 lemons
  Water
2 tablespoons peanut oil
1 medium onion, chopped
½ medium carrot, peeled and
  chopped
½ stalk celery, leaves removed and
  chopped
2 tablespoons dry sherry

1 clove garlic, chopped
5 sprigs fresh thyme
1 sprig fresh basil
1 sprig fresh tarragon
2 cups chicken stock (see page 262)
  Salt to taste
  Breaded Eggplant Rounds
  Yellow Tomato-Basil Sauce
1 small bunch chives, cut into
  2-inch pieces
¼ cup red tomatoes, peeled, cored,
  seeded, and finely diced

Soak sweetbreads overnight in cold water to cover. Drain and rinse. Place sweetbreads in a medium saucepan with salt, lemon juice, and water to barely cover. Bring to a boil over high heat. Reduce heat and simmer for 1 minute. Remove sweetbreads and plunge into a bowl of ice water until cool.

Pat dry. Peel away membranes and remove tubes, extra tissue, and fatty part.

Heat 1 tablespoon oil in a large saucepan over medium heat and sauté onion, carrot, and celery for about 4 minutes or until onion is transparent. Add sherry and garlic and cook until all liquid has evaporated. Pan should be dry.

Place herbs in pan with onion mixture and put sweetbreads on top of them. Cover with chicken stock. Bring to a boil and simmer for 12 minutes. Remove sweetbreads from liquid, cover with plastic wrap, and set aside to cool.

When cool, sweetbreads should be separated into pieces. Strain liquid and reserve 1 cup for sauce.

Prepare a smoker (see page 272).

Smoke sweetbreads for 20 minutes to take on smoky flavor.

Heat remaining 1 tablespoon oil in a large sauté pan over medium heat. Season sweetbreads to taste with salt and sauté for about 4 minutes or until golden brown and crisp. Remove and keep warm.

Place a Breaded Eggplant Round in the center of each of four warm serving plates. Spoon Yellow Tomato-Basil Sauce around the eggplant round. Fill center of round with sweetbreads. Sprinkle chives and chopped tomatoes on top of sauce and serve immediately.

BREADED EGGPLANT ROUNDS

4 ³/₄-inch-thick slices from a large
   eggplant
1 to 2 cups peanut oil
1 cup flour

Salt to taste
2 extra large eggs, lightly beaten
1 cup extra fine bread crumbs,
   sifted

Using a 3¹/₂-inch round cutter, cut a circle from the center of each eggplant slice. With a smaller cutter (approximately 2³/₄ inches around), cut out the center of each large circle, leaving four ³/₄-inch rims. (You can also use a doughnut cutter to make eggplant rounds.)

Begin heating peanut oil to 350° in a medium saucepan.

Dredge eggplant rounds in flour with salt added to taste, then in beaten eggs.

Press each round into crumbs, making sure it is completely coated. Place breaded eggplant rounds on wax paper until ready to fry.

Carefully lower eggplant rounds into hot oil one at a time. Fry 2 to 3 minutes or until golden brown. Turn and brown other side.

Drain on paper towel. Season to taste with salt. Serve immediately.

YELLOW TOMATO-BASIL SAUCE

1 tablespoon virgin olive oil
1 shallot, chopped
1 clove garlic, chopped
    Leaves of 2 to 3 sprigs fresh thyme
1 pound yellow tomatoes (red
    tomatoes may be substituted),
    chopped

1 cup reserved stock from
    sweetbreads
1/2 cup very cold unsalted butter
3 large fresh basil leaves, washed
    and dried
    Salt to taste

Heat oil in a large saucepan over medium heat and sauté shallot and garlic for about 1 minute. Add thyme, tomatoes, and stock and simmer for about 20 to 30 minutes or until mixture is thick, stirring occasionally.

Pour tomato mixture into a food processor and, using the steel blade, process until smooth.

Add butter and quickly process an additional 10 seconds (if mixture is too thick, add a small amount of chicken stock). Strain sauce.

Submerge basil in sauce and steep for at least 20 minutes. Keep warm. Add salt to taste and remove basil before serving.

Advance Preparation:
1. Sweetbreads should be soaked overnight in cold water before cooking. They may be blanched and refrigerated up to 1 day ahead.
2. Sweetbreads may be smoked several hours ahead.
3. Yellow Tomato-Basil Sauce may be prepared several hours in advance and kept warm.

 WINE SUGGESTION:

Fumé Blanc, Robert Mondavi, 1984
A medium-bodied wine with slightly spicy aromas, balanced flavors, and oak overtones to complement the subtle flavors of the smoked sweetbreads and zesty sauce.

PAN-FRIED BREADED CLAMS WITH GREEN ONION PASTA AND ROASTED GARLIC SAUCE

Serves
6

2 pounds littleneck or cherrystone
   clams in shells
2 eggs, slightly beaten
1/4 cup milk
1 large pinch cayenne pepper
1 tablespoon finely chopped fresh
   parsley

1 cup flour
1/2 cup peanut oil
   Roasted Garlic Sauce
   Green Onion Pasta
3 ounces American golden caviar

Remove clams from shell (or have fishmonger do this), reserving 1 tablespoon liquid for Roasted Garlic Sauce.

In a medium bowl, combine eggs, milk, cayenne, and parsley; whisk lightly. Add clams to liquid and marinate for 20 minutes.

Remove clams from liquid and dredge each in flour, coating evenly.

Place on wax paper and allow breading to set.

Pour oil into a large, heavy skillet over medium heat. When hot, carefully drop clams into skillet. Do not crowd skillet.

Cook on 1 side until golden brown. Turn and brown other side. Remove clams from oil and drain on paper towel. Keep warm.

Ladle Roasted Garlic Sauce over six warm serving plates. Center a small mound of Green Onion Pasta on each. Place equal portions of fried clams in a circle around the pasta. Spoon 1/2 ounce of American golden caviar into the center of pasta. Serve immediately.

ROASTED GARLIC SAUCE

3 tablespoons peanut oil
10 cloves garlic, peeled
1 tablespoon reserved clam liquid
1/4 cup white wine, preferably a
    heavy oak Chardonnay
1 tablespoon balsamic vinegar

2 cups heavy cream
3 tablespoons cold unsalted butter,
    cut into small pieces
Juice of 1/2 lemon
Salt to taste

Preheat oven to 350°. Place oil and garlic in a small ovenproof sauté pan over medium heat. Cook, stirring frequently, for about 4 minutes or until garlic cloves are evenly browned.

When brown, place pan in preheated 350° oven and cook for about 10 minutes or until cloves are soft, shaking pan every 3 minutes to prevent burning. Garlic should not be blackened but should remain a golden brown.

In a medium saucepan, combine clam liquid, wine, and vinegar. Bring liquid to a boil and cook for about 5 minutes, stirring frequently, or until liquid is reduced by one-fourth.

Add roasted garlic cloves and place in a blender with heavy cream; blend until smooth.

Whisk in butter, one piece at a time. Add lemon juice and season to taste with salt. Strain and keep warm until ready to serve.

GREEN ONION PASTA

1/3 cup chopped green onions,
    including green tops
1/2 cup water, approximately
2 cups all-purpose flour

2 tablespoons salt
1 extra large egg yolk
1 teaspoon olive oil

Place chopped green onions in a food processor. Process, using the steel blade, to the consistency of a purée, adding 1 to 2 tablespoons water until smooth.

Combine flour, 1 teaspoon salt, egg yolk, olive oil, green onion purée, and enough water to make a soft dough. Mix dough according to pasta machine manufacturer's directions. Run through pasta machine and extrude for fettuccine.

In a large pot, bring 1 gallon of water to a boil. Add remaining salt to water. Drop in pasta and stir to keep separated. Cook for 1 to 2 minutes or until just tender or al dente. Drain and use immediately.

Advance Preparation:

1. Sauce may be prepared and kept warm several hours in advance. Reheat gently if necessary.

2. Pasta may be made several hours ahead but cannot be cooked until ready to serve. Heat water for cooking pasta before frying clams.

 WINE SUGGESTION:

CHARDONNAY, TREFETHEN, 1984
A full-bodied wine with good fruit aromas and a clean, crisp taste with citrus finish to complement the clams and stand up to the rich pasta.

SMOKED RAINBOW TROUT WITH SORREL AND GRILLED TOMATO SAUCE

*Serves
4*

4 *whole medium tomatoes*
2 *tablespoons red wine vinegar*
6 *tablespoons virgin olive oil*
   Salt to taste
   Ground black pepper to taste

1 *large bunch sorrel, rinsed, dried,
   and stems removed (basil may be
   substituted)*
4 *skinless, boneless smoked rainbow
   trout fillets*

Preheat grill or light coals. Make sure grates are clean, and lightly rub or brush with vegetable oil. Over medium coals, roast whole tomatoes until skin is charred evenly on all sides. Remove from grill.

Do not peel off charred skin. Purée tomatoes in a blender. Place purée in a medium saucepan over medium heat and simmer, stirring frequently, for about 15 minutes or until liquid is reduced by half.

Strain to remove seeds. Whisk in vinegar and 6 tablespoons olive oil, pouring in a steady stream and beating constantly. Season to taste with salt and pepper. Set aside to cool to room temperature.

Arrange sorrel leaves in several stacks. Roll tightly in a cigar shape and, starting at one end, finely slice into thin chiffonade strips.

Ladle grilled tomato sauce onto four chilled serving plates, using enough to cover the entire surface. Place a bed of sorrel in the center of each plate and top with a trout fillet. Serve immediately.

Advance Preparation:
1. Grilled tomato sauce may be made the day before and refrigerated, tightly covered. Bring to room temperature before serving.
2. Sorrel leaves may be cut, wrapped in a damp towel, and refrigerated for up to 3 hours before serving.

  WINE SUGGESTION:

SAUVIGNON BLANC, FALL CREEK VINEYARDS, 1985
A dry, medium-bodied wine with floral nose and full citrus flavors to harmonize with the lemon of the sorrel and smokiness of the fish.

WILD DUCK PÂTÉ WITH PICKLED OKRA

*Serves
8*

2 wild ducks including the livers,
   skinned (if livers are unavailable,
   add 2 chicken livers)
¼ cup Madeira wine
¼ cup brandy
3 shallots, chopped
2 cloves garlic, chopped
1 teaspoon chopped fresh thyme
1 teaspoon chopped fresh cilantro
1 teaspoon chopped fresh epazote
1 teaspoon chopped fresh marigold
   mint
¾ pound sliced smoked bacon
½ red bell pepper, seeded and
   membranes removed, cut into ¼-
   inch dice (see page 271)
½ yellow bell pepper, seeded and
   membranes removed, cut in ¼-
   inch dice (see page 271)

¼ cup finely diced country ham (see
   page 271)
⅛ cup heavy cream
2 extra large eggs, lightly beaten
   Salt to taste
   Ground black pepper to taste
4 cloves garlic
3 whole serrano chilies
4 sprigs fresh sage
1 medium head red oak lettuce,
   separated, trimmed, washed, and
   dried
   Pickled Okra
⅓ cup Creole mustard

Cut duck meat from carcasses in large chunks and place in a nonmetallic container. Add livers.

Combine Madeira, brandy, shallots, chopped garlic, and chopped herbs. Pour over duck. Cover and marinate for 2 hours, turning occasionally.

Strain marinade, reserving liquid.

Preheat oven to 300°.

Grind duck, liver, shallots, garlic, herbs, and ¼ pound smoked bacon in a food grinder using a small die.

Place ground mixture in the small bowl of an electric mixer. Using the paddle blade, slowly add reserved marinade, peppers, ham, cream, and egg. Add salt and pepper to taste.

Line a 1-quart terrine or loaf pan with remaining strips of bacon, making sure strips overlap to cover top. Fill terrine with duck mixture and smooth top. Enclose top with bacon. Place garlic cloves, serrano chilies, and sprigs of sage on top of bacon. Cover tightly with aluminum foil. Place terrine in a larger pan filled with 1 inch of water. Bake in preheated 300° oven for 1 hour or until a skewer placed through the center comes out hot.

Remove terrine from oven and press down top of pâté to squeeze out excess fat. Let stand until completely cool.

Remove garlic, chilies, and sage from top and turn pâté out of terrine.

Slice pâté into ³∕₈-inch slices. Place 2 large leaves of red oak lettuce on opposite sides of each of eight cold serving plates. Overlap 2 slices of pâté in the center of each plate. Garnish 1 lettuce leaf with 4 Pickled Okra pods and the other with a dollop of Creole mustard. Serve with crisp crackers or dry toast, if desired.

NOTE: A 5-pound domestic duck with skin on may be substituted for the wild duck in this recipe. In this case, do not grind ¼ pound bacon with duck.

PICKLED OKRA

1 cup cider vinegar
½ cup water
2 tablespoons salt
2 pounds young tender okra pods, washed and dried

4 whole garlic cloves, peeled
3 whole jalapeño chilies
1 tablespoon dill seed
1 tablespoon mustard seed

Place vinegar, water, and salt in a heavy saucepan over medium heat. Bring to a boil and cook for 5 minutes.

Place remaining ingredients in a non-metallic container and pour boiling vinegar mixture over all. Cover and let cool. Stir from time to time. Refrigerate, covered, for at least 24 hours before serving.

Advance Preparation:
1. Pâté may be made up to 3 days ahead; refrigerate, tightly wrapped.
2. Pickled Okra may be made up to 1 week in advance; refrigerate, tightly covered.

 WINE SUGGESTION:

Merlot, Dehlinger, 1984
A rich, full-bodied wine with soft and polished aromas and flavors of raspberry to accompany the earthiness of the pâté.

Soups

TORTILLA SOUP

SMOKED ACORN SQUASH SOUP WITH HAZELNUT CREAM

ROASTED YELLOW BELL PEPPER SOUP WITH SERRANO CHILI CREAM

SOUTHWEST CORN CHOWDER

TEXAS BLACK BEAN AND JALAPEÑO JACK CHEESE SOUPS
WITH SMOKED RED AND YELLOW PEPPER CREAMS

YELLOW TOMATO GAZPACHO WITH SMOKED RED TOMATO CREAM

ROASTED EGGPLANT AND ROMANO CHEESE SOUP WITH BASIL CREAM

LOBSTER AND APPLE BISQUE

CAULIFLOWER CREOLE MUSTARD SOUP WITH GREEN ONIONS

CHILLED AVOCADO SOUP WITH TANGERINE-LIME SORBET

TORTILLA SOUP

*Serves
8 to 10*

Caroline Rose Hunt, creator of Rosewood Hotels and The Mansion on Turtle Creek, enjoyed this soup at the venerable Argyle Club in San Antonio and suggested its adaptation for the menu of The Mansion on Turtle Creek.

This hearty soup, which is suitable on warm spring days as well as cold winter nights, has been on the menu since The Mansion at Turtle Creek opened.

When Tortilla Soup is ordered, it is brought to the table in a tureen for individual service by the waiter, who garnishes each bowl according to the customer's desire.

3 tablespoons corn oil
4 corn tortillas, coarsely chopped
6 cloves garlic, finely chopped
1 tablespoon chopped fresh epazote
  (or 1 tablespoon chopped fresh
  cilantro)
1 cup fresh onion purée
2 cups fresh tomato purée
1 tablespoon cumin powder
2 teaspoons chili powder
2 bay leaves
4 tablespoons canned tomato purée

2 quarts chicken stock (see page
  262)
Salt to taste
Cayenne pepper to taste
1 cooked chicken breast, cut into
  strips
1 avocado, peeled, seeded, and
  cubed
1 cup shredded cheddar cheese
3 corn tortillas, cut into thin strips
  and fried crisp

Heat oil in a large saucepan over medium heat.

Sauté tortillas with garlic and epazote over medium heat until tortillas are soft. Add onion and fresh tomato purée and bring to a boil. Add cumin, chili powder, bay leaves, canned tomato purée, and chicken stock. Bring to a boil again, then reduce heat to simmer. Add salt and cayenne pepper to taste and cook, stirring frequently, for 30 minutes. Skim fat from surface, if necessary.

Strain and pour into warm soup

bowls. Garnish each bowl with an equal portion of chicken breast, avocado, shredded cheese, and crisp tortilla strips. Serve immediately.

Advance Preparation:
1. Soup may be made 1 day ahead and gently reheated before serving.

Smoked Acorn Squash Soup with Hazelnut Cream

*Serves
6 to 8*

4 acorn squash, halved and seeded
1 large onion, coarsely chopped
4 tablespoons unsalted butter
½ cup dry sherry
1 quart chicken stock (see page 262)
   Sachet (1 bay leaf, 5 sprigs fresh
   thyme, 1 tablespoon white
   peppercorns tied in a cheesecloth
   bag)

1 cup heavy cream
Salt to taste
White pepper to taste
Lemon juice to taste
Hazelnut Cream

Smoke 4 squash halves for 20 minutes (see page 272).

Preheat oven to 350°.

Remove squash from smoker and place, with remaining squash halves, in a flat pan, cut side down. Bake in pre-heated 350° oven for 1 hour or until soft. Scoop out pulp and set aside.

In a medium saucepan, sauté onion in butter over medium heat until soft. Add squash pulp and stir in sherry. Pour in chicken stock and add sachet. Simmer for approximately 1 hour or until flavors mellow and light smoked flavor from squash becomes distinct. Remove sachet.

Pour into a blender and blend until very smooth. Return to saucepan and stir in cream. Bring to a simmer and cook for about 20 minutes or until soup has thickened. Season to taste with salt, pepper, and lemon juice.

Pour equal portions into warm soup bowls. Garnish with a dollop of Hazelnut Cream or swirl cream over surface of soup. Serve immediately.

HAZELNUT CREAM

2 ounces shelled hazelnuts
½ cup very cold heavy cream

1 teaspoon hazelnut oil
Salt to taste

Preheat oven to 350°.

Spread hazelnuts on sheet tray and place in preheated 350° oven for 6 minutes or until golden, shaking tray every 2 minutes to ensure even roasting.

When done, pour nuts on one-half of a thick kitchen towel and fold over other half. Rub nuts together between two layers of towel to remove skins. This procedure will remove most, but not all, of the skin. Expect a small amount to remain.

Place roasted, skinned hazelnuts in a food processor. With the steel blade, using on-off motion, finely chop nuts.

They should be a fine texture, as if ground. *Do not overprocess to a nut butter.*

Whip cream to soft peaks. (This may also be done in the food processor, but remove nuts first.)

Fold ground hazelnuts and oil into cream. Season to taste with salt, if desired. Use immediately.

Advance Preparation:

1. Smoked Acorn Squash Soup may be prepared up to 1 day in advance, covered tightly, and refrigerated. Gently reheat just before serving.

ROASTED YELLOW BELL PEPPER SOUP
WITH SERRANO CHILI CREAM

*Serves
6 to 8*

Craig Claiborne, in Dallas to judge a gourmet gala, was invited to lunch at the restaurant in which I was chef. He didn't want to attend, but the owner sent a limousine and he came, "just for a drink." Once there, the owner, Lawrence Herkimer, insisted he stay, "just for the first course." He reluctantly agreed, but "I really must go then." As we got ready to serve the soup, the maître d' panicked—"the cream is too spicy, you're going to ruin our big moment." Silence reigned as we all waited for America's premiere food critic's reaction. "I'm from Mississippi and I haven't had a good, spicy soup since I left." He stayed through the entire lunch and even came back to do a feature story on me in the New York Times. *My first national recognition came from this soup!*

4 yellow bell peppers
2 tablespoons peanut oil
1 large onion, chopped
2 large shallots, chopped
2 cloves garlic, chopped
3/4 cup dry sherry
2 yellow tomatoes, peeled, seeded, and chopped (1 pint yellow cherry tomatoes may be substituted)
1 quart chicken stock (see page 262)

Sachet (1 bay leaf, 1 tablespoon black peppercorns, 3 sprigs fresh thyme, 1 sprig fresh basil, 1 large sprig fresh parsley tied in cheesecloth bag)
1 cup heavy cream
Juice of 1/2 lemon
Salt to taste
Ground black pepper to taste
Serrano Chili Cream

Roast yellow bell peppers until skin turns black (see page 261). Place in a plastic bag and secure end. Allow peppers to "steam" for 10 minutes. Remove

from bag. Pull off skin, cut peppers in half, and remove seeds; chop coarsely and set aside.

Heat oil in a large saucepan over

medium heat and sauté onion, shallots, and garlic. Add sherry and cook for about 15 minutes or until liquid evaporates. Add tomatoes, chicken stock, and sachet and cook for about 10 minutes or until liquid is reduced by one-third. Add cream and peppers. Bring to a simmer and cook for about 15 minutes or until liquid is slightly reduced. Remove sachet.

Place soup in a blender and blend until very smooth.

Strain through a fine sieve and season to taste with lemon juice, salt, and pepper. If necessary, gently reheat. (Or, if desired, cover and refrigerate for at least 3 hours and serve as a cold soup.)

Pour equal portions into warm soup bowls. Garnish each with a dollop of Serrano Chili Cream. Swirl cream over surface of soup. Serve immediately.

SERRANO CHILI CREAM

3 serrano chilies, seeded and stems removed
1 clove garlic, peeled
1 shallot, peeled
5 medium-sized spinach leaves, stems removed

1/2 cup very cold heavy cream
Juice of 1/2 lime
Salt to taste

Combine chilies, garlic, and shallot in a small saucepan. Cover with water and bring to a boil. Lower heat and simmer for 10 minutes. Drain and place in a blender along with spinach. Blend until puréed.

Pour cream into the bowl of a food processor and, using the plastic blade, whip to soft peaks. (You can also whip cream with an electric mixer.) Fold puréed chilies into cream. Season to taste with lime juice and salt. Use immediately.

Advance Preparation:
1. Roasted Yellow Bell Pepper Soup may be prepared up to 1 day in advance, covered tightly, and refrigerated. Gently reheat just before serving.

SOUTHWEST CORN CHOWDER

Serves
6

6 *large ears sweet corn*
1 *teaspoon corn oil*
2 *onions, cut into medium dice*
2 *cloves garlic, chopped*
1¹/₂ *poblano chilies, seeded and*
  chopped into medium dice
2 *serrano chilies, seeded and*
  chopped
3 *cups chicken stock (see page 262)*
2 *cups heavy cream*
  Salt to taste
1 *tablespoon lime juice,*
  approximately

1 *small baking potato, peeled and*
  cut into medium dice (see page
  271)
¹/₂ *cup jicama, peeled and cut into*
  medium dice (see page 271)
¹/₄ *red bell pepper, seeded and*
  membranes removed, cut into
  medium dice (see page 271)
¹/₄ *yellow bell pepper, seeded and*
  membranes removed, cut into
  medium dice (see page 271)
1 *tablespoon finely chopped fresh*
  cilantro

Shuck corn, remove silk, and cut kernels from cob. Set aside ³/₄ cup.

Heat oil in a heavy saucepan over medium heat. Stir in remaining corn kernels and onions. Sauté for about 10 minutes or until onions are soft and juices have cooked down. *Do not brown.*

Add garlic, 1 chopped poblano, 1 chopped serrano chili, and chicken stock. Bring to a boil, stirring frequently. Reduce heat and simmer for 20 minutes.

Stir in cream. Return soup to a simmer and cook for about 5 minutes or until slightly reduced.

Remove from heat. Pour soup into a blender and blend until very smooth. Season to taste with salt and lime juice. Set aside and keep warm.

Fill a large pot three-quarters full with water. Bring to a boil. Season lightly with salt.

Add potato and cook for 2 minutes. Add reserved ³/₄ cup corn kernels and cook for 2 minutes. Add jicama, bell peppers, and remaining diced poblano and serrano chilies; cook for 2 minutes.

Drain vegetables and immediately fold into warm soup. Pour equal portions into six warm soup bowls. Sprinkle an equal amount of chopped cilantro on each and serve immediately.

Advance Preparation:

1. Entire soup may be made up to 1 day in advance. Reheat, but *do not cook*, just before serving.

Texas Black Bean and Jalapeño Jack Cheese Soups with Smoked Red and Yellow Pepper Creams

*Serves
6*

The look on the diner's face tells the story of this soup. The reaction is as though to a piece of contemporary art, as if it weren't meant to be eaten. A design is created by swirling red and yellow pepper creams on the half-black, half-white background composed of the black bean and cheese soups.

*Black Bean Soup
Jalapeño Jack Cheese Soup*

*Smoked Red and Yellow Pepper
Creams*

Prepare soups and creams. When done, simultaneously pour ladlesful of hot Black Bean Soup and Jalapeño Jack Cheese Soup into wide, warm soup bowls. Pour gently so that soups meet in the center of the soup bowls but *do not mix.*

Using squeeze bottles, streak Red Pepper Cream over the surface of the Jalapeño Jack Soup and Yellow Pepper Cream over the surface of the Black Bean Soup. The effect should be similar to a modern painting. Serve immediately.

BLACK BEAN SOUP

1 cup dry black beans
1 onion, chopped
3 cloves garlic, chopped
1 jalapeño chili, seeded and chopped
1 small leek (white part only), chopped
1 stalk celery, chopped

4 sprigs fresh cilantro
1 quart chicken stock (see page 262)
1 cup ham scraps or 1 large ham bone
Salt to taste
Ground black pepper to taste
Juice of 1 lemon

Rinse beans and discard any that are shriveled. Cook beans in cold water to cover for 2 to 3 hours; drain.

Place soaked beans, onion, garlic, chili, leek, celery, cilantro, chicken stock, and ham in a large stock pot and bring to a boil over high heat. Lower heat and simmer for about 2 hours or until beans are very soft, skimming off foam frequently.

When beans are soft, remove ham scraps or bone. Pour beans into a blender or food processor (divide in batches if necessary) and blend until smooth. Strain and season to taste with salt, pepper, and lemon juice. Soup should be thick, but if it is too thick, thin with additional hot chicken stock.

JALAPEÑO JACK CHEESE SOUP

2 tablespoons vegetable oil
1 onion, chopped
1 small leek (white part only), chopped
1 stalk celery, chopped
2 cloves garlic, chopped
1½ cups flat beer
½ cup white wine
1 quart chicken stock (see page 262)
1 jalapeño chili, seeded and chopped

Sachet (1 bay leaf, 5 sprigs fresh thyme, 1 tablespoon white peppercorns tied in cheesecloth bag)
2 tablespoons softened unsalted butter
2 tablespoons flour
1 cup shredded jalapeño Jack cheese
¼ cup heavy cream
Salt to taste
Ground black pepper to taste
Juice of 1 lemon

Heat oil in a large sauté pan over medium heat. Sauté onion, leek, celery, and garlic for about 5 minutes or until soft.

Add beer and wine and bring to a boil. Cook for about 10 minutes or until liquid is reduced by half.

Add chicken stock, jalapeño chili, and sachet. Bring to a boil. Skim foam from top, lower heat, and simmer for about 1 hour. Remove sachet.

Knead together butter and flour. Slowly whisk into soup and blend until smooth.

Simmer for an additional 30 minutes.

Remove from heat and immediately stir in cheese and heavy cream and blend with whisk until smooth.

Place liquid in a blender or food processor (in batches if necessary to accommodate size of container) and blend mixture until smooth. Strain and season to taste with salt, pepper, and lemon juice. Soup should be very thick, but if it is too thick, thin with additional hot chicken stock.

SMOKED RED AND YELLOW PEPPER CREAMS

1 red bell pepper, stems and seeds
 removed
¼ cup very cold heavy cream
½ cup sour cream

Salt to taste
Lime juice to taste
1 yellow bell pepper, stems and
 seeds removed

Smoke peppers 20 minutes to take on smoke flavor (see page 272).

To make Red Pepper Cream, in a food processor, using the steel blade, or a blender, purée smoked red pepper until very smooth. Add 2 tablespoons cream and ¼ cup sour cream. Process briefly to combine. Season to taste with salt and lime juice. Strain through a fine sieve.

Pour into a squeeze bottle with a tube-type top (the kind used by beauticians or as catsup or mustard containers in diners and coffee shops) and set aside.

Clean bowl of food processor and repeat the process using smoked yellow pepper and remaining ingredients. Pour into another squeeze bottle and set aside.

Advance Preparation:
1. Soups may be prepared up to 1 day ahead and refrigerated. Reheat and adjust seasoning and thickness just before serving.
2. Smoked creams may be prepared several hours ahead and refrigerated until ready to serve.

Yellow Tomato Gazpacho
with Smoked Red Tomato Cream

*Serves
6 to 8*

*2 pounds ripe yellow tomatoes,
  coarsely chopped*
*¹/₂ large cucumber, peeled, seeded,
  and coarsely chopped*
*¹/₂ large yellow bell pepper, seeded
  and coarsely chopped*
1 clove garlic, minced
1 shallot, minced
¹/₂ tablespoon minced fresh cilantro
¹/₂ tablespoon minced fresh basil

1 serrano chili, seeded and chopped
*1 tablespoon white wine vinegar or
  to taste*
Salt to taste
Juice of 1 lime
*Few drops of pure maple syrup, if
  needed*
Smoked Red Tomato Cream
6 to 8 fresh cilantro leaves

Using a food grinder with a medium die, grind tomatoes, cucumber, bell pepper, garlic, shallot, cilantro, basil, and serrano chili, catching all juices as you grind. Or process vegetables in small batches in a food processor using the steel blade. Vegetables should be of even size and finely chopped but not puréed.

Combine vegetables and juices in a medium bowl. Add vinegar and season to taste with salt and lime juice. If soup tastes slightly bitter, add a few drops of maple syrup.

Cover bowl tightly with plastic wrap and refrigerate for at least 2 hours before serving. Soup should be very cold.

Pour equal portions into chilled bowls and garnish with a dollop of Smoked Red Tomato Cream and a cilantro leaf.

SMOKED RED TOMATO CREAM

*½ pound ripe red tomatoes, stem
    area removed*
1 shallot, minced
1 clove garlic, minced

1 serrano chili, seeded and minced
½ cup very cold heavy cream
    Salt to taste
    Juice of ½ lime, or to taste

Cut tomatoes in half and smoke for 15 minutes (see page 272).

Combine smoked tomatoes, shallot, garlic, and serrano chili in a small saucepan over low heat. Use a wooden spoon to break up tomatoes and release juices.

Bring mixture to a slow boil and simmer, stirring constantly, for 10 to 12 minutes or until very thick.

Using a fine sieve, strain tomato mixture into a small bowl, forcing as much of the juice through the strainer as possible. Cool completely, then refrigerate to chill.

In a medium bowl, whip cream to form soft peaks. Fold in cold tomato mixture. Season to taste with salt and lime juice. Cover and keep cold until ready to serve.

Advance Preparation:
1. Yellow Tomato Gazpacho can be made up to 2 days in advance, covered tightly, and refrigerated.
2. Smoked red tomato juice for Smoked Red Tomato Cream can be made up to 2 days in advance, covered tightly, and refrigerated. It should not be added to whipped cream more than 1 hour before using.

Roasted Eggplant and Romano Cheese Soup with Basil Cream

*Serves
6 to 8*

*1 large eggplant
2 tablespoons vegetable oil
1 large onion, chopped
1 shallot, chopped
2 cloves garlic, chopped
2 serrano chilies, 1 seeded and
   chopped and 1 chopped with
   seeds*

*1 small bunch fresh thyme, tied
   together
1 quart chicken stock (see page 262)
1 cup heavy cream
1/2 cup grated Romano cheese
   Salt to taste
   Juice of 1/2 lemon
   Basil Cream*

Place whole eggplant in a large, dry, cast-iron skillet over medium heat. Slowly cook eggplant for about 15 minutes or until charred on all sides turning frequently. Do not be concerned if skin of eggplant burns. The eggplant should look as though it has been deflated. Remove eggplant from heat and let stand until cool enough to handle.

Under cool running water, carefully remove charred skin and stem. Reserve pulp of eggplant for soup.

Heat oil in a large saucepan over medium heat and sauté onion for about 5 minutes or until soft. Add shallot, garlic, and chilies. Sauté for 1 minute. Add thyme and chicken stock. Bring liquid to a boil and cook for about 30 minutes or until reduced by half.

Stir in cream and bring to a hard boil for 3 minutes, stirring occasionally.

Remove thyme from liquid. Stir in eggplant and cheese and bring to a boil.

Remove from heat and process mixture in a blender or food processor until smooth. Process in batches, if necessary, to accommodate size of container. Strain through a fine sieve and return to saucepan. Heat through. Season to taste with salt and lemon juice.

Pour equal portions into warm soup bowls. Garnish with a dollop of Basil Cream and serve immediately.

BASIL CREAM

6 *leaves fresh basil, stems removed*
3 *leaves spinach, stems removed*
1 *tablespoon cold water*

¼ *cup heavy cream*
  Salt to taste
  Lemon juice to taste

Combine basil, spinach, and water in a blender or food processor. Use just enough cold water to moisten the leaves to make a smooth purée.

Whip cream to soft peaks and gently fold in basil mixture. Season to taste with salt and lemon juice. Whip again with wire whisk to thicken, if necessary. Use immediately.

Advance Preparation:
1. Roasted Eggplant and Romano Cheese Soup may be made up to 1 day in advance, covered tightly, and refrigerated. Gently reheat just before serving.

LOBSTER AND APPLE BISQUE

*Serves
6 to 8*

1 2-pound live Maine lobster
2 tablespoons virgin olive oil
1 tablespoon sesame oil
1 medium yellow onion, chopped
1 small carrot, peeled and chopped
1 small stalk celery, leaves removed
  and sliced
½ cup tomato paste
2 pounds Granny Smith apples,
  peeled, cored, and coarsely
  chopped (in season, substitute 2
  pounds yellow-fleshed plums,
  peeled, pitted, and coarsely
  chopped)
¼ cup plum wine
¼ cup white port wine
 2 tablespoons finely grated fresh
  ginger

2 cloves garlic, finely chopped
2 green onions, trimmed and
  chopped
  Bouquet garni (1 sprig each fresh
  tarragon, thyme, parsley, basil,
  and cilantro tied together)
1 tablespoon whole black
  peppercorns
1 teaspoon cayenne pepper
1 quart chicken stock (see page 262)
2 tablespoons softened unsalted
  butter
2 tablespoons flour
2 cups heavy cream
  Salt to taste
  Juice of 1 lime

Preheat oven to 400°.

Plunge a sharp, pointed knife into the center back of the lobster, where the body meets the tail, to kill it. Disjoint lobster, removing tail and claws from body. Clean away remnants of intestinal vein and stomach sac from tail portion. Rinse. (The fishmonger can also do this for you.)

Heat olive oil in a large ovenproof sauté pan over medium-high heat. Sauté lobster tails and claws (in shells) for about 3 minutes or until pieces start to turn red. Place sauté pan in preheated 400° oven and cook lobster for 7 minutes. Remove lobster from oven and let stand until cool enough to handle.

Pull all lobster meat from claws and tails. Do not discard shells. Keep all pieces of lobster shell for soup preparation. Cut lobster meat into a fine dice and reserve.

Heat sesame oil in a large saucepan over medium-high heat and sauté onion, carrot, and celery for about 4 minutes or until onion is transparent. Do not allow vegetables to brown.

Add lobster shell and tomato paste to saucepan. Cook for 4 minutes.

Add apples, plum wine, port, ginger, and garlic. Cook for about 8 minutes or until liquid has evaporated, stirring occasionally. Lower heat as liquid reduces, being careful not to burn solid ingredients.

Add green onions, bouquet garni, peppercorns, cayenne, and stock. Bring soup to a simmer and cook for 1 hour.

Strain soup through a medium sieve into a large, clean pot. Use a ladle or spatula to push as much of the solids as possible through the sieve. Return to heat, blend butter and flour and whisk into soup, and simmer for 20 minutes.

Stir in cream. Season to taste with salt and lime juice. Remove from heat. Strain again; add lobster meat, heat through, and serve immediately in warm, flat soup bowls.

CAULIFLOWER CREOLE MUSTARD SOUP WITH GREEN ONIONS

*Serves
6 to 8*

1 medium onion, chopped
1 stalk celery, chopped
2 cloves garlic, chopped
2 shallots, chopped
3 cups raw cauliflower florets,
   chopped
2 tablespoons vegetable oil
¹/₂ cup white port wine
¹/₂ cup sherry
1 quart chicken stock (see page 262)
   Sachet (1 bay leaf, 5 sprigs fresh
   thyme, 1 tablespoon white
   peppercorns tied in a cheesecloth
   bag)

¹/₄ cup Creole mustard
   Juice of 1 lemon
   Salt to taste
   Ground black pepper to taste
1 teaspoon Worcestershire sauce, or
   to taste
¹/₄ teaspoon Tabasco sauce, or to
   taste
1 cup heavy cream
1 bunch green onions, finely
   chopped

In a large saucepan over medium heat, sauté onion, celery, garlic, shallots, and cauliflower in oil for about 5 minutes or until onion is transparent.

Stir in port and cook over high heat for about 5 minutes or until liquid is reduced by half.

Add sherry and cook for about 3 minutes or until liquor bouquet dissipates.

Add chicken stock and sachet, bring to a boil, then simmer for about 30 minutes or until liquid is reduced by half. Remove sachet.

Pour soup into a blender and blend until very smooth. Strain through a fine sieve and return to heat. Stir in mus-tard. Season to taste with lemon juice, salt, pepper, and Worcestershire and Tabasco sauces.

Whisk in cream and heat through, but do not allow to boil. Pour equal portions into warm serving bowls. Garnish with chopped green onions and serve immediately.

Advance Preparation:
1. Without the final addition of heavy cream, soup may be made up to 2 days in advance, tightly covered, and refrigerated. Reheat and stir in heavy cream just before serving.

CHILLED AVOCADO SOUP WITH TANGERINE-LIME SORBET

*Serves
6 to 8*

1 *shallot, minced*
1 *clove garlic, minced*
1 *serrano chili, stemmed and minced*
1 *tablespoon unsalted butter*
1 *quart chicken stock (see page 262)*
5 *spinach leaves, rinsed, dried, and
　stems removed*

4 *small (or 2 very large) avocados,
　peeled, seeded, and coarsely
　chopped*
Juice of 1 lemon
Salt to taste
Tangerine-Lime Sorbet

In a large saucepan, sauté shallot, garlic, and chili in butter for 2 minutes. Add chicken stock and bring to a boil. Immediately remove from heat. Add spinach and avocados.

Purée in a blender or food processor until very smooth. Strain through a fine sieve.

Add lemon juice and salt to taste. Cover tightly and refrigerate for at least 3 hours.

When cold, ladle into individual soup bowls. Garnish with a small scoop of Tangerine-Lime Sorbet and serve immediately.

TANGERINE-LIME SORBET

2 *cups fresh strained tangerine juice
　Juice of 2 limes*

¹/₄ *cup simple syrup (see page 268)
　Zest of 2 tangerines*

Combine all ingredients and pour into the container of an ice cream freezer. Freeze according to manufacturer's directions.

Advance Preparation:
1. Chilled Avocado Soup may be made up to 8 hours in advance, covered tightly, and refrigerated. Blend before serving.
2. Tangerine-Lime Sorbet may be made up to 24 hours in advance.

Salads

SMOKED TEXAS GAME BIRDS WITH SOUTHWEST VEGETABLES
AND MEXICAN MARIGOLD MINT VINAIGRETTE

SPICY FRIED OYSTERS ON ROASTED PEPPERS
WITH SPINACH AND RADICCHIO SALAD

WARM QUAIL SALAD WITH HONEY-MUSTARD VINAIGRETTE

CRAB SALAD WITH MEXICAN VEGETABLES
AND CORIANDER-CUMIN VINAIGRETTE

SMOKED SALMON SALAD WITH DILL SABAYON SAUCE
AND TOMATO-CAPER RELISH

TEMPURA SNOW PEA SALAD WITH SPINACH AND ARUGULA,
SERVED WITH ORIENTAL MUSTARD-BALSAMIC VINAIGRETTE

SMOKED PHEASANT SALAD WITH ANCHO-HONEY VINAIGRETTE
AND SPICY FRIED PASTA

WARM SHRIMP AND SCALLOP PASTA SALAD

MANSION SALAD WITH FRESH HERB VINAIGRETTE
AND CHEESE CROUTONS

SMOKED TEXAS GAME BIRDS WITH SOUTHWEST VEGETABLES AND MEXICAN MARIGOLD MINT VINAIGRETTE

*Serves
4*

2 cups julienne strips smoked game
  birds (pheasant, duck, quail,
  squab; see page 272)
1/2 red bell pepper, seeded and
  membranes removed, cut into
  julienne strips
1/2 yellow bell pepper, seeded and
  membranes removed, cut into
  julienne strips
1/2 carrot, peeled and cut into
  julienne strips
1/2 small jicama, peeled and cut into
  julienne strips
1/2 small zucchini, (only part that has
  green skin attached) cut into
  julienne strips
1 dried pear half, cut into fine
  julienne strips

2 tablespoons chopped fresh
  Mexican marigold mint (or 1
  tablespoon chopped fresh mint
  and 1 tablespoon chopped fresh
  tarragon)
1 shallot, minced
1 clove garlic, minced
1 tablespoon lemon juice
3 tablespoons white wine vinegar
1/2 cup plus 1 tablespoon peanut oil
  Salt to taste
  Ground black pepper to taste
  Mexican marigold mint or mint
  leaves for garnish, if desired

Toss together julienne strips of game, vegetables, and dried pear.

In a separate small mixing bowl, whisk together marigold mint, shallot, garlic, lemon juice, vinegar, oil, salt, and pepper. Pour over julienne ingredients and toss to blend.

Place a small mound of salad in the middle of four salad plates. Garnish with Mexican marigold mint or mint leaves, if desired.

NOTE: This salad may also be used as a main course luncheon dish garnished with Spicy Fried Pasta (see page 12).

Advance Preparation:
1. Game birds and vegetables may be cut into julienne strips several hours before serving.

 WINE SUGGESTION:

Sauvignon Blanc, Robert Pepi, 1984
A crisp, full-bodied wine with lemon nose and well-balanced, slightly herbal taste to help marry the flavors of the complex dish.

Spicy Fried Oysters on Roasted Peppers with Spinach and Radicchio Salad

Serves 4

16 medium-large fresh oysters
2 cups dried corn-bread crumbs
1 serrano chili, seeded and finely chopped
1 clove garlic, finely chopped
1 teaspoon cayenne pepper

1 teaspoon ground black pepper
1/2 cup peanut oil
  Spinach and Radicchio Salad with Balsamic Vinaigrette
  Roasted Peppers

Shuck oysters and reserve their juice (or have the fishmonger do this for you).

In a medium bowl, combine crumbs, serrano chili, garlic, cayenne pepper, and black pepper, mixing well.

Lift oysters out of juice, one at a time, and dredge in crumb mixture to coat heavily. Strain and reserve 1 tablespoon oyster liquor for vinaigrette.

Place breaded oysters on wax paper until ready to fry.

Heat oil in a large sauté pan over medium heat.

Carefully place oysters in pan, one at a time. Brown for 2 minutes, turn, and brown other side for about 2 minutes. Do not overcook. Remove and keep warm.

Mound Spinach and Radicchio Salad in the center of four luncheon plates. Place four small mounds of Roasted Peppers at equal intervals around each salad. Place a fried oyster on each mound of peppers. Spoon a small pool of balsamic vinaigrette between each oyster and serve immediately.

SPINACH AND RADICCHIO SALAD WITH BALSAMIC VINAIGRETTE

1 anchovy fillet
1 small clove garlic, chopped
1 small shallot, chopped
2 teaspoons Dijon mustard
3 tablespoons balsamic vinegar
1 teaspoon egg yolk
1 teaspoon chopped fresh basil
1 teaspoon chopped fresh dill
1 teaspoon chopped fresh thyme
1 cup peanut oil

1 tablespoon virgin olive oil
1 tablespoon reserved oyster liquor, strained
Juice of 1/2 lemon or to taste
Salt to taste
1/4 pound spinach leaves, rinsed and dried
1 small head radicchio, rinsed and dried

In a blender or food processor, combine anchovy, garlic, shallot, mustard, vinegar, egg yolk, and herbs. Process until smooth.

With motor running, pour peanut oil in a thin, steady stream into anchovy mixture. Add olive oil and oyster liquor to blend. Season to taste with lemon juice and salt. Set aside.

Pick over spinach leaves, removing any bruised or discolored ones. Stack ten spinach leaves on top of one another and roll into a cigar shape.

Using a sharp knife, start at one end of the "cigar" and cut 1/4-inch strips. Carefully unroll the spinach into a large bowl. Repeat with the remaining spinach.

Remove the core from the head of radicchio. Roll and cut leaves into 1/4-inch strips as for spinach.

Toss spinach and radicchio with just enough balsamic vinaigrette to coat lightly. Reserve remaining dressing for presentation.

ROASTED PEPPERS

2 *red bell peppers*
1 *yellow bell pepper*
1 *green bell pepper*
   Juice of 1 lemon
3 *tablespoons virgin olive oil*
1 *clove garlic, minced*

1 *small shallot, minced*
   Leaves of 4 sprigs fresh thyme,
   minced (stems discarded)
   Salt to taste
   Ground black pepper to taste

Roast peppers until black on all sides (see page 261). Place peppers in a plastic bag and seal the end. Let them steam for 20 minutes. Pull off skin and remove stem and seeds. Spread each pepper in a single layer and slice into fine julienne strips.

Place pepper strips in a medium bowl and add lemon juice, oil, garlic, shallot, and thyme. Mix well and season to taste with salt and pepper. Cover and set aside for at least 1 hour to marinate.

Advance Preparation:
1. Peppers may be roasted and mari-nated several days ahead, covered tightly, and refrigerated. Remove from refrigerator 1 hour before serving.
2. Vinaigrette may be prepared several hours ahead, covered, and kept cool.
3. Chiffonade of spinach and radicchio may be prepared several hours in advance, loosely wrapped in damp paper towels, and stored in a plastic bag in refrigerator crisper. Be careful not to crush. Toss with vinaigrette just before serving.
4. Fry oysters just before serving.

 WINE SUGGESTION:

CHARDONNAY, CHÂTEAU BOUCHAINE, LOS CARNEROS, 1984
A full-bodied wine with a spicy nose and a crisp, slightly buttery taste to contrast the radicchio and spicy vinaigrette.

WARM QUAIL SALAD WITH HONEY-MUSTARD VINAIGRETTE

Serves
4

This is a favorite salad served at The Mansion on Turtle Creek. The unique combination of a cold salad of greens with roasted quail and a warm dressing of sweet and sour flavors provides a contrast in texture, taste, and temperature.

4 6- to 7-ounce quail
Salt to taste
The Mansion on Turtle Creek
Pepper Mixture to taste (see page 261)
4 tablespoons safflower oil
1/4 cup chopped onion
1/4 cup chopped celery
1/4 cup chopped carrot
1 bay leaf
4 sprigs fresh thyme
1 tablespoon cracked black pepper
2 cups veal demi-glace (see page 263)
1/2 small head Bibb lettuce, leaves separated, rinsed, and dried

1/2 small head radicchio, leaves separated, rinsed, and dried
1/2 carrot, peeled
3 bundles mâche lettuce, rinsed well to remove all grit and leaves separated and dried
1/2 small head chicory, yellow leaves only, rinsed, dried, and torn
1/2 bag or bundle enoki mushrooms, cut from stems (optional)
2 tablespoons sherry vinegar
2 tablespoons virgin olive oil
3 tablespoons peanut oil
Salt to taste
Honey-Mustard Vinaigrette

Preheat oven to 400°.

Remove wings and wishbone from quail (see page 149). Season quail inside and out with salt and Pepper Mixture to taste.

In a medium ovenproof sauté pan over medium-high heat, sear quail on all sides in 2 tablespoons safflower oil. Without removing from sauté pan,

place quail in preheated 400° oven and cook for 8 minutes. Remove from oven and set aside.

In a large saucepan, sauté onion, celery, and carrot in remaining 2 tablespoons safflower oil for about 10 minutes or until golden brown. Remove from heat and set aside.

Cut legs from quail. Using the sharp

tip of a knife, remove breast meat from carcass. Reserve legs and breast halves; keep warm.

Add quail carcasses to sautéed vegetables, along with bay leaf, thyme, and pepper. Add demi-glace to cover. Place saucepan over high heat and bring to a boil. Skim foam from top and simmer for 30 minutes.

Strain off vegetables and carcasses and discard. Reserve 1 cup remaining demi-glace for use in vinaigrette.

Tear Bibb lettuce into bite-sized pieces. Remove the core from the head of radicchio, stack and roll leaves into a cigar shape, and cut into thin slices. Cut carrot into thin julienne strips.

In a large salad bowl, combine Bibb lettuce, radicchio, carrot, mâche lettuce, chicory, and mushrooms.

In a small bowl, combine vinegar and olive and peanut oils. Add salt to taste and pour over greens. Gently toss until well mixed.

Place equal portions of seasoned salad greens on four luncheon plates. Slice quail breasts into julienne strips and place on top of greens, allowing 2 halves per serving. Place quail legs in crisscross pattern at top of plate. Spoon Honey-Mustard Vinaigrette over the Quail Salad and serve immediately. This salad may also be used as a luncheon main course.

NOTE: If French green beans are available, they may be blanched, then rinsed in cold water and used as a garnish around the outside edge of the salad.

HONEY-MUSTARD VINAIGRETTE

3 tablespoons Dijon mustard
2 tablespoons honey
1 tablespoon safflower oil
2 tablespoons minced shallots
4 tablespoons honey vinegar or white wine vinegar

1 cup reserved quail demi-glace
Salt to taste
Ground black pepper to taste

Mix mustard and honey. Set aside.

In a small saucepan, heat oil and sauté shallots for about 2 minutes or until transparent. Add vinegar and cook for about 5 minutes or until almost all liquid has evaporated.

Add reserved quail demi-glace and bring to a boil. Stir in mustard and honey mixture and remove from heat.

Season with salt and pepper to taste. Keep warm.

Advance Preparation:

1. Vegetables for salad may be prepared several hours ahead, wrapped in damp paper towel, placed in plastic bags, and refrigerated. Toss with vinegar-oil dressing just before serving.

2. Vinaigrette may be prepared up to 1 hour in advance and kept warm.

 WINE SUGGESTION:

CHARDONNAY, LLANO ESTACADO, LEFTWICH-SLAUGHTER, 1984
A dry, medium-bodied wine with apple and honey nose and crisp, tart finish to provide balance to the quail and the sweet-sour dressing.

CRAB SALAD WITH MEXICAN VEGETABLES AND CORIANDER-CUMIN VINAIGRETTE

*Serves
4*

¹/₂ *pound jumbo lump crabmeat*
¹/₂ *red bell pepper, seeded and
    membranes removed*
¹/₂ *yellow bell pepper, seeded and
    membranes removed*
¹/₂ *poblano chili, seeded and
    membranes removed*
¹/₂ *small jicama, peeled*

¹/₂ *medium carrot, peeled*
¹/₂ *small chayote squash, peeled and
    pit removed (any hard, crisp
    squash may be substituted)
    Coriander-Cumin Vinaigrette
    Whole fresh cilantro leaves for
    garnish*

Pick over crab to remove any traces of shell.

Cut bell peppers and poblano into thin julienne strips, about 1¹/₂ inches long. Cut jicama, carrot, and chayote into julienne strips of equal size.

Toss together crab, julienne vegeta-bles, and Coriander-Cumin Vinaigrette to coat all ingredients.

Place equal portions of Crab Salad with Mexican Vegetables on four cold salad plates, mounding in the center. Garnish sparingly with whole cilantro leaves. Serve immediately.

CORIANDER-CUMIN VINAIGRETTE

1 small mango, peeled and pit
  removed (¹/₂ papaya may be
  substituted)
1 tablespoon diced smoked red bell
  pepper (see pages 271 and 272)
1 teaspoon ground cumin
1 teaspoon ground dried coriander
1 tablespoon chopped fresh cilantro
1 serrano chili, seeded and finely
  chopped

1 clove garlic, chopped
1 small shallot, chopped
2 teaspoons grated fresh ginger
1 tablespoon maple syrup or to taste
  Juice of 1 lime
1¹/₂ cups peanut oil
  Salt to taste

Combine all ingredients except oil and salt in a food processor or blender. Process until mixture is smooth.

With motor running, pour oil in a thin, steady stream into container until mixture has thickened and begins to emulsify. Season to taste with salt. Strain and chill thoroughly. Use one-third for salad; reserve remainder for other salads or vegetables. May be stored, refrigerated and tightly covered, for up to 1 week.

Advance Preparation:
1. Crab salad may be made several hours ahead of time, mixed with vinaigrette, covered, and refrigerated.

 WINE SUGGESTION:

Semillon, Clos du Val, 1984
A medium-bodied wine with an oak fig nose and rich, lean taste with a touch of butterscotch to contrast with the spicy vinaigrette on the salad.

SMOKED SALMON SALAD WITH DILL SABAYON SAUCE AND TOMATO-CAPER RELISH

*Serves
6*

*½ pound very thinly sliced smoked
salmon
1 red bell pepper, seeded and
membranes removed
1 green bell pepper, seeded and
membranes removed
1 yellow bell pepper, seeded and
membranes removed*

*1 zucchini
1 yellow squash
1 carrot, peeled
Dill Sabayon Sauce
¼ pound fresh spinach leaves
Tomato-Caper Relish*

Cut salmon and peppers into fine julienne strips.

Trim peel, including about ¼ inch of the vegetable, from zucchini and yellow squash. You should have ¼-inch-thick strips of peel the length of the vegetable. Cut peels into pieces approximately the same length as other julienne strips, then cut into fine julienne. Reserve remaining zucchini and squash for another use.

Cut carrot into thin julienne strips the same size as other vegetables. Toss together salmon and julienne vegetables. Slowly add Dill Sabayon Sauce and toss lightly to coat.

Stem, rinse, and dry spinach. Remove any blemished leaves. Then stack 10 spinach leaves on top of one another and roll into a cigar shape. Using a sharp knife, start at one end and cut ¼-inch slices all the way to the other end of the spinach roll. Carefully unroll strips of spinach into a small bowl. Repeat with remaining spinach.

Mound equal portions of Smoked Salmon Salad in the center of six luncheon plates. Place three small piles of chiffonade of spinach around salad at equal intervals. Place about 1 tablespoon of Tomato-Caper Relish on each spinach pile. Serve immediately.

DILL SABAYON SAUCE

1 anchovy
1 clove garlic, chopped
1 tablespoon Dijon mustard
2 tablespoons balsamic vinegar
1 teaspoon egg yolk
1 small bunch fresh dill, stems removed (about ¹/₄ cup loosely packed)

1 cup peanut oil
1 tablespoon virgin olive oil
¹/₄ cup heavy cream
  Salt to taste
  Juice of ¹/₂ lemon or to taste

Combine anchovy, garlic, mustard, vinegar, egg yolk, and dill in a blender or food processor and process until smooth.

With motor still running, pour a thin stream of peanut and olive oils into container. Process just until mixture begins to thicken and emulsify. (It will begin to take on a shine.)

With motor running, add cream and immediately turn off machine. Ingredients should be incorporated but cream should not be beaten.

With a rubber spatula, stir in salt and lemon juice to taste. Just before serving, thin with a few drops of water to achieve a sauce the consistency of heavy cream.

TOMATO-CAPER RELISH

1 clove garlic, finely chopped
1 shallot, finely chopped
2 tablespoons chicken stock (see page 262)
2 tablespoons white wine vinegar
1½ tablespoons caper juice
1 tablespoon brown sugar

1 tablespoon pickling spice, tied in cheesecloth
¼ cup diced red onion
1 tablespoon drained capers
2 ripe tomatoes, peeled, cored, seeded, and diced

Combine garlic, shallot, chicken stock, vinegar, caper juice, brown sugar, and pickling spice in a small saucepan over medium heat. Bring to a boil and cook about 2 minutes or until almost all liquid has evaporated. About 2 tablespoons should remain. Remove pickling spice and pour remaining liquid into a medium bowl.

Add onion and capers.

Drain excess juice from tomatoes and add to other ingredients. Toss, cover, and marinate at least 1 hour.

Advance Preparation:

1. Salad may be tossed with dressing and refrigerated up to 1 hour in advance. Allow salad to reach near room temperature before serving.
2. Chiffonade of spinach may be prepared several hours ahead. Wrap in damp paper towel, seal in plastic bag, and store in refrigerator to hold.
3. Sabayon may be made several hours in advance and refrigerated, covered.
4. Tomato-Caper Relish may be prepared up to 24 hours in advance, covered, and refrigerated.

 WINE SUGGESTION:

CHARDONNAY, McDOWELL VALLEY, 1984
A full-bodied wine with a stony, oaky nose and lean, elegant apple taste to accompany the smoky flavors of the salmon and the rich sabayon sauce.

Tempura Snow Pea Salad with Spinach and Arugula, Served with Oriental Mustard-Balsamic Vinaigrette

Serves
6

2 bunches arugula
1 pound fresh spinach
1 pint yellow cherry tomatoes
5 cups peanut oil
½ cup flour
½ cup cornstarch
2 extra large eggs, separated

1 cup soda water
Salt to taste
Cayenne pepper to taste
¾ pound fresh snow peas, rinsed,
dried, and stems removed
Oriental Mustard-Balsamic
Vinaigrette

Rinse arugula and spinach. Select pretty, unblemished leaves and pat dry. Set aside.

Rinse and dry tomatoes. Set aside.

Begin heating oil to 350° in a medium saucepan. Combine flour, cornstarch, egg yolks, and soda water, mixing well. If mixture seems too thin, add a bit more flour and cornstarch.

Whip egg whites to soft peaks and fold into batter mixture. Season to taste with salt and cayenne pepper.

When oil is hot, dip dry snow peas into batter mixture, coating well. Drop into hot oil, being careful not to crowd pan. Fry for 2 minutes or until golden brown. Drain on paper towel and keep warm.

Ladle small amount of Oriental Mustard-Balsamic Vinaigrette onto six salad plates. On half of each plate, arrange hot tempura snow peas in a fan shape. On the other side of each plate, arrange leaves of greens in a similar fan shape. Place 2 to 3 cherry tomatoes in the center. Serve immediately.

ORIENTAL MUSTARD-BALSAMIC VINAIGRETTE

1 tablespoon finely grated fresh
  ginger
½ tablespoon minced fresh garlic
1½ tablespoons finely chopped green
  onions
1 jalapeño chili, seeded and finely
  chopped

¼ cup balsamic vinegar
2 tablespoons Dijon mustard
1 teaspoon egg yolk
¾ cup peanut oil
1 teaspoon lime juice
  Salt to taste

Combine ginger, garlic, green onions, jalapeño, vinegar, mustard, and egg yolk; whisk together vigorously until well incorporated.

Whisking constantly, add oil in a steady stream until mixture is emulsified. Season to taste with lime juice and salt. If too thick, thin with a few drops of water.

Advance Preparation:
1. Spinach and arugula leaves may be rinsed and dried up to 1 day ahead. Refrigerate between layers of damp paper towel in plastic bags.
2. Dressing may be prepared several hours before serving. Refrigerate to store; serve at room temperature.

 WINE SUGGESTION:

SAUVIGNON BLANC, ALDERBROOK, 1985
A medium-bodied wine with a slightly oaky nose and full, fruity flavor to contrast the greens and spicy dressing.

SMOKED PHEASANT SALAD WITH ANCHO-HONEY VINAIGRETTE AND SPICY FRIED PASTA

Serves
6

1 *2¹/₂-pound smoked and fully cooked pheasant (see page 272)*
1 *red bell pepper, seeded, membranes removed, and cut into fine julienne strips*
1 *yellow bell pepper, seeded, membranes removed, and cut into fine julienne strips*
1 *carrot, peeled and cut into fine julienne strips*
1 *small jicama, peeled and cut into fine julienne strips*
1 *small zucchini (only part that has green skin attached), cut into julienne strips*

1 *teaspoon minced fresh tarragon*
1 *teaspoon minced fresh parsley*
1 *teaspoon minced fresh thyme*
1 *teaspoon minced fresh chives*
1 *teaspoon minced fresh basil*
1 *shallot, minced*
1 *clove garlic, minced*
2 *tablespoons white wine vinegar*
6 *tablespoons peanut oil*
  Ancho-Honey Vinaigrette
  Spicy Fried Pasta (see page 12)

Remove skin from pheasant and cut breast and thigh meat only into fine julienne strips.

Combine pheasant strips with bell peppers, carrot, jicama, and zucchini.

In a small bowl, combine herbs, shallot, garlic, vinegar, and oil. Whisk mixture until well incorporated and toss thoroughly with pheasant mixture to coat all ingredients.

Spread Ancho-Honey Vinaigrette on six salad plates. Place equal portions of Smoked Pheasant Salad in small mounds in the middle of each plate. Surround each mound with strips of Spicy Fried Pasta.

ANCHO-HONEY VINAIGRETTE

4 ancho chilies, seeded and stems
    removed
2 shallots
2 cloves garlic, peeled
1 small bunch cilantro
2 cups water

$^1/_3$ cup honey
$^1/_4$ cup white wine vinegar
  1 tablespoon balsamic vinegar
$^1/_2$ cup peanut oil
    Juice of $^1/_2$ lime or to taste
    Salt to taste

Preheat oven to 400°.

Lay ancho chilies flat in a single layer on a baking sheet. Place in preheated 400° oven for 2 minutes. Remove from oven, allow to cool enough to handle, and pull off peel.

Combine anchos, shallots, garlic, and cilantro in a small saucepan. Cover with water. Bring liquid to a boil and cook for about 10 minutes or until reduced by two-thirds.

Pour ancho mixture into a blender or food processor and process until very smooth. Add honey and vinegars; blend again until smooth.

While blender or processor is running, slowly add peanut oil in a thin, steady stream until all oil is incorporated. Add lime juice and salt to taste.

Advance Preparation:
1. Pheasant may be smoked up to 1 or 2 days ahead; refrigerate, tightly covered.
2. Vinaigrette may be prepared up to 1 day ahead and refrigerated. Process or blend before serving if refrigerated.

 WINE SUGGESTION:

CHARDONNAY, MANZANITA, 1983
A full-bodied wine with a spicy nose and rich honey-oak flavors to complement the smoked pheasant and its spicy sweet dressing.

WARM SHRIMP AND SCALLOP PASTA SALAD

*Serves
8*

3 tablespoons peanut oil
½ pound medium shrimp (16 to 20
  per pound), peeled and deveined
½ pound scallops
  Salt to taste
1 red bell pepper, seeded,
  membranes removed, and cut into
  julienne strips
1 yellow bell pepper, seeded,
  membranes removed, and cut into
  julienne strips
1 small carrot, peeled and cut into
  julienne strips
1 small jicama, peeled and cut into
  julienne strips
1 small zucchini (only part that has
  green skin attached), cut into
  julienne strips
2 halves dried pears, cut into fine
  julienne strips

½ pound tricolor rotelle, cooked and
  drained
1 tablespoon finely chopped fresh
  chervil
1 tablespoon finely chopped fresh
  basil
½ tablespoon finely chopped fresh
  thyme
1 tablespoon finely chopped fresh
  chives
½ tablespoon finely chopped fresh
  parsley
1 shallot, minced
1 clove garlic, minced
3 tablespoons white wine vinegar
½ cup peanut oil
  Ground black pepper to taste
  Juice of ½ lemon or to taste

Heat oil in a medium sauté pan over medium-high heat.

Season shrimp and scallops lightly with salt. Sauté shrimp for 2 minutes, add scallops, and sauté 2 more minutes. Remove from heat and keep warm.

Toss together vegetables, pear halves, and rotelle. Set aside. Combine herbs, shallot, garlic, vinegar, and oil; mix well. Add vinegar mixture, shrimp, and

scallops to pasta mixture and toss well to blend.

Season to taste with additional salt, pepper, and lemon juice.

Place equal portions on eight salad plates and serve immediately.

Advance Preparation:

1. Pasta may be cooked and drained several hours ahead and tossed lightly

with a very small amount of peanut oil. Cover and keep at room temperature.

2. Vegetables and pear may be cut into julienne strips and refrigerated several hours before serving. Remove from refrigerator 30 minutes before serving.

3. Salad dressing may be prepared several hours before use. Cover and keep at room temperature.

 WINE SUGGESTION:

CHARDONNAY, NEYERS, 1985
A medium-bodied wine with lemony overtones and a touch of oak with the freshness to complement this light springtime dish.

Mansion Salad with Fresh Herb Vinaigrette and Cheese Croutons

Serves 8

1 small head Boston or Bibb lettuce
1 small head red oak lettuce or ra-
    dicchio
2 bundles mâche lettuce
1 head baby white chicory

1 head Belgian endive
4 red baby pear tomatoes
4 yellow baby pear tomatoes
    Fresh Herb Vinaigrette
    Cheese Croutons

Rinse, core, dry, and separate all lettuces into a large bowl. Separate, wash, and dry endive leaves and set aside. Wash and dry tomatoes and set aside.

Toss all lettuces with Fresh Herb Vinaigrette.

Place 2 Belgian endive leaves at the 12 o'clock position on each of eight salad plates to form a V. Place a red and yellow tomato on each side of the V. Place equal portions of salad on each plate. Place Cheese Croutons opposite the Belgian endive and serve immediately.

FRESH HERB VINAIGRETTE

1 large shallot, minced
1 large clove garlic, minced
1 teaspoon minced fresh basil
1 teaspoon minced fresh thyme
1 teaspoon minced fresh parsley
1 teaspoon minced fresh tarragon
1 teaspoon minced fresh chives

1½ tablespoons white wine vinegar
1 teaspoon balsamic vinegar
4 tablespoons peanut oil
1 tablespoon virgin olive oil
    Juice of ½ lemon
    Salt to taste

Combine shallot, garlic, herbs, and vinegars in a small bowl. Whisk in oils.

Season to taste with lemon juice and salt. Mix well to blend.

CHEESE CROUTONS

8 ½-inch-thick slices from a French
   baguette
2 ounces fresh goat cheese
2 ounces white cheddar cheese

2 ounces Brie
2 tablespoons heavy cream
   Salt to taste
   Cayenne pepper to taste

Preheat oven to 375°.

Place bread slices on a baking sheet and toast until bread just begins to brown. Turn and toast just until surface begins to dry.

In a food processor, using the steel blade, blend goat cheese, cheddar, Brie, and cream until smooth. Mix in salt and pepper to taste.

Spread a small amount of cheese mixture on each toast slice. Return to broiler just long enough to melt cheese. Serve warm.

Advance Preparation:

1. Vinaigrette may be prepared up to 1 day ahead. Refrigerate covered to store but serve at room temperature.
2. Rinse salad leaves several hours ahead. Wrap loosely in damp paper towels. Place in a plastic bag and refrigerate until just before serving. Dry thoroughly before using.
3. Croutons may be toasted and cheese blended a few hours ahead. Melt cheese on croutons just before serving.

Main Courses

Fish

GRILLED GULF RED SNAPPER WITH TOMATILLO—SERRANO
CHILI VINAIGRETTE AND CORN-BREAD OYSTERS

PAN-FRIED RED SNAPPER WITH SAUCE OF SWEET CORN, LEEK,
DALLAS MOZZARELLA, AND CRABMEAT

PAN-FRIED GULF RED SNAPPER WITH SERRANO CHILI—CILANTRO
SAUCE AND BLACK BEAN RELISH

GRILLED SWORDFISH WITH MANGO, CUCUMBER, MELON,
AND LIME SAUCE

PAN-FRIED SWORDFISH WITH TEQUILA-TOMATO VINAIGRETTE
AND JICAMA SALAD

GRILLED SWORDFISH WITH PINEAPPLE—RED CHILI SALSA

GRILLED SWORDFISH STEAKS WITH CUCUMBER-GINGER
VINAIGRETTE AND FRIED CABBAGE

NORWEGIAN SALMON WITH A CRUST OF FOUR PEPPERCORNS
ON A BED OF MATCHSTICK VEGETABLES

SEARED SALMON WITH HORSERADISH POTATOES AND HARD-BOILED
EGG—CAPER SAUCE

HALIBUT WITH ORANGE HORSERADISH CRUST
AND THAI SHRIMP SALAD

HALIBUT BREADED WITH CASHEWS SERVED WITH MANGO-BASIL SAUCE

GRILLED REDFISH WITH ARTICHOKE-OYSTER SAUCE
AND CRISP SHOESTRING YAMS

SOLE FILLETS WITH MACADAMIA NUT CRUST WITH
PAPAYA-BASIL SAUCE

Grilled Gulf Red Snapper
with Tomatillo–Serrano Chili Vinaigrette
and Corn-Bread Oysters

Serves 4

Using all regional ingredients, this recipe represents a refinement of Southwest cuisine—light but satisfying with the hot snapper served on a room-temperature vinaigrette.

4 7-ounce red snapper fillets, trimmed
  of skin and bones
3 tablespoons peanut oil
  Salt to taste

Ground black pepper to taste
Tomatillo–Serrano Chili Vinaigrette
Corn-Bread Oysters

Prepare fire for grilling (see page 275). Make sure grates are clean and lightly rub or brush with oil just before placing fish on grill.

Dip fillets in 3 tablespoons peanut oil and place on preheated grill, skin side up. Season skin side with salt and pepper to taste. Grill snapper about 2 minutes, just long enough to mark one side. Turn fillets and season lightly with salt and pepper. Cook fillets another 2 min-

utes or just until fish feels firm. Do not overcook. The fish should be very moist.

Ladle Tomatillo–Serrano Chili Vinaigrette over the bottom of each of four warm dinner plates. Place a red snapper fillet in the middle of each plate. Arrange 3 Corn-Bread Oysters in a triangle pattern at even intervals near the rim of each plate. Serve immediately.

TOMATILLO—SERRANO CHILI VINAIGRETTE

1 pound tomatillos, husks removed, diced (see page 271)
½ cup diced jicama (see page 271)
½ cup diced mango (see page 271)
2 tablespoons diced red bell pepper (see page 271)
2 tablespoons diced yellow bell pepper (see page 271)
2 serrano chilies, seeded and finely chopped

1 cup peanut oil
2 tablespoons virgin olive oil
¼ cup white wine vinegar
2 tablespoons balsamic vinegar
Juice of ½ lime
2 teaspoons lemon juice
¼ cup chopped fresh cilantro
1 clove garlic, minced
Salt to taste

Combine tomatillos, jicama, mango, red and yellow peppers, and serrano chilies in a medium bowl.

In another bowl, combine peanut and olive oils, vinegars, and lime and lemon juices. Blend in cilantro, garlic, and salt to taste.

Pour over tomatillo mixture and stir to blend.

CORN-BREAD OYSTERS

3 cups peanut oil
1½ cups yellow cornmeal
½ cup flour
2 teaspoons baking powder
1 teaspoon salt or to taste
2 extra large eggs, lightly beaten

¼ cup bacon grease, melted
2 cups milk
About 2 tablespoons fresh oyster liquor
12 shucked fresh oysters

Place oil in a deep-sided pot and heat to 375°. Lightly stir together cornmeal, flour, baking powder, and salt.

Add eggs, bacon grease, and milk. Add just enough oyster liquor (about 2 tablespoons) to make mixture the consistency of corn-bread batter. Stir until smooth. The batter should not be too thick or too thin. If too thick, add a bit more milk. If too thin, add a bit more cornmeal. Dip each oyster into batter and carefully lower into hot oil. Do not crowd the pan. Add just enough oysters to form a single layer without touching. (You will have excess batter, which can be stored, refrigerated, and tightly covered for up to 3 days and may be used for breading vegetables and other fish.)

Fry until golden brown on both sides. Remove from oil. Drain on paper towel and keep warm.

Advance Preparation:
1. Vinaigrette may be prepared several hours ahead and held at room temperature.
2. Oysters may be fried and kept warm while grilling snapper.

 WINE SUGGESTION:

SAUVIGNON BLANC, ROBERT PECOTA, 1985
Crisp, medium-bodied, full-flavored wine with lemon-lime taste and a touch of oak provides a balance to this highly seasoned but light dish.

PAN-FRIED RED SNAPPER WITH SAUCE OF SWEET CORN, LEEK, DALLAS MOZZARELLA, AND CRABMEAT

Serves
4

4 *tablespoons peanut oil*
4 *7-ounce red snapper fillets, trimmed*
   of skin and bones
   Salt to taste

Sauce of Sweet Corn, Leek, Dallas
Mozzarella, and Crabmeat
1 *small bunch fresh chives, washed,*
   dried, and cut into 2-inch segments

Heat oil in a large skillet over medium heat. Season each fillet with salt. Pan-fry fillets on flesh side until a heavy crust forms, being careful not to burn them.

Turn fillets and cook just until no longer translucent. Allow no more than 5 minutes total cooking time for each ½ inch of thickness at the thickest part. Do not overcook. The fish should be very moist.

Spoon just enough Sauce of Sweet Corn, Leek, and Dallas Mozzarella to cover the bottom of each of four warm dinner plates. Place a red snapper fillet in the middle of each plate. Sprinkle sweet corn, leek, pepper, and crabmeat around each fillet, then sprinkle each serving with chive segments. Serve immediately.

SAUCE OF SWEET CORN, LEEK, DALLAS MOZZARELLA, AND CRABMEAT

1 tablespoon corn oil
2 cups fresh sweet corn kernels
1 shallot, chopped
1 clove garlic, chopped
1 serrano chili, seeded and chopped
3 sprigs fresh cilantro
2 sprigs fresh thyme
2 cups chicken stock (see page 262)
1/2 cup heavy cream
1 ounce Dallas mozzarella (or other fresh mozzarella cheese)

Salt to taste
Lemon juice to taste
2 tablespoons unsalted butter
1 leek, white part only, cut into thin julienne strips
1/2 red bell pepper, seeds and membrane removed, cut into a fine dice (see page 271)
4 ounces jumbo lump crabmeat

Heat oil in a medium saucepan over medium heat. Sauté 1 cup corn kernels, shallot, garlic, and serrano chili for 3 minutes.

Add cilantro, thyme, and chicken stock. Simmer for 20 minutes. Stir in cream and bring to a boil. Cook for about 15 minutes or until liquid is reduced by half, stirring occasionally.

Pour into a blender. Add mozzarella and process until smooth. Strain through a fine sieve and season to taste with salt and lemon juice. Keep warm until ready to use.

Melt butter in a sauté pan over medium heat and add remaining 1 cup corn kernels, leek, and pepper. Sauté until vegetables soften. Add crabmeat and heat through. Keep warm until ready to use.

Advance Preparation:
1. Sauce may be prepared up to 1 hour ahead and kept warm.
2. Ready garnish ingredients for cooking several hours ahead; sauté up to 1 hour before serving. Keep warm.

 WINE SUGGESTION:

SPARKLING WINE, IRON HORSE BRUT, 1983
A lean, slightly yeasty, sparkling wine with tart citrus finish provides contrast to the creamy sweetness of the sauce and complements the delicacy of the fish.

Pan-Fried Gulf Red Snapper with Serrano Chili–Cilantro Sauce and Black Bean Relish

Serves
4

This is one of the first Southwest recipes I developed using regional ingredients. It brings back good memories of the trial-and-error days with my old crew. It remains a favorite on The Mansion on Turtle Creek menu.

4   6-ounce red snapper or redfish fillets, trimmed of skin and bones
   Salt to taste

6   *tablespoons peanut oil*
   Serrano Chili–Cilantro Sauce
   Black Bean Relish

Season fish to taste with salt. Heat oil in a large skillet or sauté pan over medium heat. Carefully place fillets in pan, presentation side down.

Brown slowly for 2 to 3 minutes so fillets are cooked almost completely through. Turn and finish cooking for about 2 minutes.

Carefully remove fish from pan and blot any excess oil with a paper towel.

Place a fish fillet on each of four warm dinner plates. Spoon Serrano Chili–Cilantro Sauce around each fillet. Place a small mound of Black Bean Relish beside each fillet and serve immediately.

SERRANO CHILI—CILANTRO SAUCE

3 small serrano chilies, seeded and
  sliced
2 shallots, minced
3 garlic cloves, minced
2 cups chicken stock (see page 262)
2 cups heavy cream

1/2 cup cilantro leaves, large stems
  removed
4 medium spinach leaves
  Juice of 1/2 lime or to taste
  Salt to taste

Combine serrano chilies, shallots, garlic, chicken stock, and cream in a medium saucepan. Bring to a boil, lower heat, and simmer for about 20 to 25 minutes or until liquid is reduced by half.

Pour into a blender or food processor. Add cilantro and spinach leaves and process until very smooth. Strain through a fine sieve.

Season to taste with lime juice and salt. Keep warm until ready to use.

BLACK BEAN RELISH

1 meaty smoked ham bone,
  approximately 1 pound
1/2 cup chopped onion
1/4 cup chopped celery
1/4 cup chopped carrot
1 bay leaf
1 tablespoon black peppercorns
3 serrano chilies
2 small jalapeño chilies
3 cloves garlic
1/2 small bunch cilantro plus 2
  tablespoons chopped fresh
  cilantro
2 1/2 cups chicken stock (see page 262)
3/4 cup dried turtle or black beans,
  rinsed and picked over

1 small red bell pepper, stemmed,
  seeded, and membranes removed,
  cut into small dice (see page 271)
1 small yellow bell pepper,
  stemmed, seeded, and membranes
  removed, cut into small dice (see
  page 271)
2 tablespoons white wine vinegar
1 tablespoon balsamic vinegar
1 tablespoon virgin olive oil
  Salt to taste
  Juice of 1 lemon or to taste
  Juice of 1 lime or to taste

In a large stock pot, combine ham bone, onion, celery, carrot, bay leaf, peppercorns, serrano chilies, 1 small jalapeño chili, 2 cloves garlic, 1/2 small bunch cilantro, and chicken stock. Bring to a boil, skim, and simmer for 1 hour or until ham flavor is dominant. Strain through a fine sieve and set aside, reserving liquid. You should have 2 cups of liquid.

Place beans in a medium saucepan with 2 cups ham stock or enough to cover by about 2 inches. Bring liquid to a boil, reduce heat, and simmer for about 45 minutes or until beans are tender but not soft. Drain beans and combine, while still hot, with bell peppers, 2 tablespoons chopped cilantro, and vinegars and oil.

Mince remaining clove garlic and jalapeño chili and stir into beans. Season to taste with salt and lemon and lime juices. Let cool to room temperature before serving.

Advance Preparation:
1. Relish may be prepared up to 1 day ahead, covered and refrigerated. Bring to room temperature to serve.
2. Sauce may be prepared up to 2 hours before serving and kept warm.

 WINE SUGGESTION:

ZINFANDEL, JOSEPH PHELPS, 1985
A light-bodied wine with lively fruit flavors and low tannins should be served chilled (60°) and will provide the strength and character to complement this robust dish.

GRILLED SWORDFISH WITH MANGO, CUCUMBER, MELON, AND LIME SAUCE

*Serves
6*

3 tablespoons peanut oil
6 7-ounce center-cut swordfish fillets,
   trimmed of fat, skin, and dark
   membrane

Salt to taste
Mango, Cucumber, Melon, and
Lime Sauce

Preheat grill or prepare coals (see page 275). When ready to cook, make sure grates are clean and lightly rub or brush with peanut oil.

Place 3 tablespoons peanut oil in a small bowl. Dip fillets in oil and season both sides with salt.

Place fillets on preheated grill. Cook for about 2 minutes on one side. Turn and cook for 2 to 3 more minutes or until fish is no longer translucent. Allow no more than 5 minutes total cooking time for each ½ inch of thickness at the thickest part. Do not overcook. The fish should be very moist. Remove from fire but keep warm.

Ladle Mango, Cucumber, Melon, and Lime Sauce over the bottom of each of six warm dinner plates. Place swordfish fillets in center and serve immediately.

MANGO, CUCUMBER, MELON, AND LIME SAUCE

1 mango
½ cucumber
¼ medium cantaloupe
¼ medium honeydew melon
½ small red bell pepper, inner
   membranes removed
½ small yellow bell pepper, inner
   membranes removed
½ cup white port wine
½ cup white wine vinegar

2 shallots, finely chopped
1 clove garlic, finely chopped
2 tablespoons grated fresh ginger
½ cup heavy cream
1½ cups very cold unsalted butter cut
   into small pieces
   Salt to taste
   Juice of 1 lime or to taste
3 to 4 basil leaves, tied together

Peel, seed, and cut into medium dice (see page 271) the mango, cucumber, cantaloupe, honeydew melon, and bell peppers. Combine in a medium bowl. Cover and set aside.

Combine port, vinegar, shallots, garlic, and ginger in a small saucepan over medium heat. Bring to a boil and cook for about 10 minutes or until liquid has almost completely evaporated. Add cream and cook for about 3 minutes or until thick.

Remove saucepan from heat and whisk in butter, piece by piece, until completely incorporated.

Drain accumulated juices from diced fruit mixture. Strain butter mixture through a fine sieve into the bowl with the diced fruit mixture. Stir to incorporate; season with salt and lime juice to taste. Add basil leaves and steep for at least 10 minutes before serving, then remove. Keep warm in the top half of a double boiler over low heat.

Advance Preparation:
1. Fruits and vegetables for sauce may be diced several hours ahead.
2. Sauce may be prepared ahead to point of adding butter. Reheat sauce and whisk in butter just before serving.

 WINE SUGGESTION:

CHARDONNAY, SONOMA CUTRER, RUSSIAN RIVER RANCHES, 1985
A full-bodied wine with aromas of tropical fruit and lemon and a rich, crisp flavor to complement the fruity citrus sauce and grilled aspects of the fish.

PAN-FRIED SWORDFISH WITH TEQUILA-TOMATO VINAIGRETTE AND JICAMA SALAD

*Serves
6*

6 8-ounce swordfish steaks,
  *trimmed of fat, skin, and dark
  membrane*
  Salt to taste

Season swordfish to taste with salt.

Heat oil in a large sauté pan over high heat. Sauté swordfish for 3 minutes. Reduce heat to medium, turn swordfish, and sauté for 2 minutes or until no longer translucent. Allow no more than 5 minutes total cooking time for each ½ inch of thickness at thickest part. Do not overcook. The fish should be very moist.

½ cup peanut oil
  Tequila-Tomato Vinaigrette
  Jicama Salad
12 *large leaves cilantro for garnish*

Ladle Tequila-Tomato Vinaigrette over the bottom of each of six dinner plates. Place 1 swordfish steak in the center of each plate. Mound a small amount of Jicama Salad at the top of the plate. Garnish with 2 large leaves of cilantro on either side of swordfish. Serve immediately.

TEQUILA-TOMATO VINAIGRETTE

½ cup tequila
¼ cup white wine vinegar
 1 shallot, minced
 1 clove garlic, minced
¼ cup virgin olive oil
½ cup diced tomatillos

Combine tequila, vinegar, shallot, and garlic in a small saucepan over medium heat. Bring to a boil and cook for about 15 minutes or until liquid is reduced by half.

1 *cup peeled, cored, seeded, and
  diced tomatoes (see page 271)*
2 *tablespoons finely chopped fresh
  cilantro*
  Salt to taste
  Ground black pepper to taste

Remove from heat and whisk in olive oil, pouring in a thin stream. Add tomatillos, tomatoes, and cilantro. Season to taste with salt and pepper. Cover and set aside until ready to use.

JICAMA SALAD

1 *small jicama, peeled and cut into
   julienne strips*
3 *tablespoons lime juice*
2 *tablespoons finely chopped fresh cilantro*

Salt to taste
Cayenne pepper to taste

Combine jicama and lime juice in a medium bowl. Add cilantro and toss together lightly, being careful not to break jicama. Season to taste with salt and pepper. Cover and set aside until ready to use.

Advance Preparation:
1. Vinaigrette may be prepared several hours ahead and held at room temperature.
2. Jicama may be cut into julienne strips up to 1 day ahead and refrigerated, tightly covered. (It will not discolor.) Combine with other ingredients at room temperature up to 2 hours before serving.

 WINE SUGGESTION:

CHARDONNAY, MONTICELLO, CORLEY VINEYARDS, 1984
*Full-bodied wine with sweet oak and lemon flavors to complement the
tomato and jicama and provide a rich, long finish for the tequila.*

GRILLED SWORDFISH WITH PINEAPPLE–RED CHILI SALSA

Serves
6

My friend Jonathan Waxman, owner of three innovative restaurants in New York City, served me a similar salsa at Bud's. I loved the flavor and came back to recreate my version for our menu.

3 tablespoons sesame oil
6 7-ounce swordfish steaks, trimmed
    of fat, skin, and dark membrane

Salt to taste
Pineapple–Red Chili Salsa

Preheat grill or light coals (see page 275). Make sure grates are clean, and lightly rub or brush with vegetable oil before placing fish on grill. Brush steaks with 3 tablespoons sesame oil and season to taste with salt.

Place steaks on preheated grill and cook for about 2 minutes or just long enough to mark 1 side. Turn and cook for about 2 minutes or until fish is firm. Allow no more than 5 minutes total cooking time for each 1/2 inch of thickness at the thickest part. Do not overcook. The fish should be moist.

Ladle Pineapple–Red Chili Salsa over the bottom of each of six warm dinner plates. Place swordfish steaks in the center and serve immediately.

PINEAPPLE—RED CHILI SALSA

*½ very ripe pineapple, cored and
  chopped*
½ mango (or papaya), chopped
½ red bell pepper, chopped
½ yellow bell pepper, chopped
¼ jicama, chopped
½ tablespoon grated fresh ginger
1 clove garlic, minced
1 serrano chili, seeded and minced
*2 dried cayenne chilies, seeded and
  minced (or ⅛ teaspoon ground
  cayenne pepper)*

2 teaspoons minced fresh cilantro
2 teaspoons minced fresh basil
2 teaspoons minced fresh mint
1 tablespoon white wine vinegar
*1 tablespoon sweet rice wine
  vinegar*
1 teaspoon soy sauce
1 teaspoon sesame oil
Salt to taste
Juice of 1 lime or to taste

Put pineapple, mango, bell peppers, ji-cama, ginger, garlic, and serrano and cayenne chilies through small die of a food grinder to make a medium-sized chunk consistency. Ingredients should not be puréed.

Combine fruits and vegetables with their juices with herbs, vinegars, soy sauce, oil, salt, and lime juice. Marinate for 2 hours before serving. Serve at room temperature.

Advance Preparation:
1. Salsa may be prepared early in the day or at least 2 hours before serving.

 WINE SUGGESTION:

Chenin Blanc, Chateau Ste. Michelle, 1985
*A fresh, clean wine with a peppery-melon nose and a fruity, off-dry
finish to complement the spicy fruit sauce and grilled flavor of the fish.*

Grilled Swordfish Steaks
with Cucumber-Ginger Vinaigrette and Fried Cabbage

*Serves
4*

4 *7-ounce swordfish steaks, trimmed
   of fat, skin, and dark membrane*
2 *tablespoons dark sesame oil
   Salt to taste*

*Cucumber-Ginger Vinaigrette
Fried Cabbage*
1 *tablespoon black sesame seeds, if
   available*

Preheat grill or light coals (see page 275). Make sure grates are clean and lightly rub or brush with vegetable oil just before placing steaks on grill.

Brush both sides of swordfish steaks with 2 tablespoons dark sesame oil. Season with salt to taste and place on preheated grill.

Cook for about 2 minutes to mark one side. Turn steaks and cook for about 2 minutes longer. Allow about 5 minutes total cooking time for each ½ inch of thickness at the thickest part. Do not overcook. The steaks should be very moist.

Arrange sliced, marinated cucumbers from Cucumber-Ginger Vinaigrette in a circle around the edge of each of four warm dinner plates. Place 1 swordfish steak in the center of each plate. Stir Cucumber-Ginger Vinaigrette and spoon over fish. Place a small mound of Fried Cabbage on each plate. Sprinkle with black sesame seeds. Serve immediately.

CUCUMBER-GINGER VINAIGRETTE

½ seedless English cucumber, sliced
  ⅛ inch thick, unpeeled
1 clove garlic, finely chopped
1 small shallot, finely chopped
1 tablespoon finely grated fresh
  ginger
1 serrano chili, seeded and finely
  chopped
3 sprigs fresh cilantro, finely
  chopped
1 medium leaf fresh basil, finely
  chopped

½ small red bell pepper, seeded,
  membranes removed, and finely
  diced (see page 271)
½ small yellow bell pepper, seeded,
  membranes removed, and finely
  diced (see page 271)
½ cup sweet rice wine vinegar
½ cup chicken stock (see page 262)
1 teaspoon sesame oil
1 teaspoon soy sauce
  Salt to taste
  Juice of ½ lime or to taste

Toss together cucumber, garlic, shallot, ginger, serrano chili, cilantro, basil, and bell peppers. Stir together vinegar, chicken stock, sesame oil, and soy sauce. Mix with vegetables. Season to taste with salt and lime juice. Marinate for 2 hours.

Before using, remove cucumber slices and reserve for garnish.

FRIED CABBAGE

4 cups peanut oil
2 cups loosely packed, finely shredded
  cabbage, core removed

Salt to taste

In a very deep saucepan heat oil to 350°.

Plunge small batches of cabbage into hot oil (*being very careful not to splatter oil*), using a slotted spoon to separate pieces. It will cook to light brown in less than 45 seconds. Quickly remove to paper towels.

Lightly season to taste with salt and serve immediately.

Advance Preparation:
1. Cucumber-Ginger Vinaigrette may be prepared up to 2 hours ahead.

 WINE SUGGESTION:

CHARDONNAY, ST. ANDREWS, 1984
A tart, clean wine with overtones of lemon and oak provides complement to the acidic salsa and the smoky flavor of the sesame oil.

Norwegian Salmon with a Crust of Four Peppercorns on a Bed of Matchstick Vegetables

*Serves
6*

6 7-ounce salmon fillets, skin and
  bones removed
  Salt to taste
2 tablespoons black peppercorns
2 tablespoons white peppercorns
2 tablespoons dried green
  peppercorns
2 tablespoons dried red peppercorns

2 tablespoons mustard seeds
3 tablespoons peanut oil
  Matchstick Vegetables
12 leafy mâche lettuce sprigs, rinsed
   well and dried (fresh watercress
   sprigs may be substituted)

Season fillets on both sides with salt. Place all peppercorns and mustard seeds in a coffee (or nut) grinder and process until roughly cracked. Spread peppercorn mixture on a small plate or wax paper. Press one side of each fillet into the pepper mixture.

Heat oil in a large sauté pan over medium heat. When oil is hot, add fillets, peppered side down, cooking no more than 2 or 3 at a time, depending on size of pan. Do not crowd pan and do not allow pan to cool too much with each addition.

Sauté salmon for 2 minutes to form a crust of peppercorns. *Do not blacken.* Carefully turn and cook for 2 more minutes or just until fish flakes. Allow approximately 4 minutes cooking time for each ½ inch of thickness at the thickest part. Do not overcook. The fish should be moist.

Arrange equal portions of Matchstick Vegetables on each of six warm dinner plates to cover the bottom of the plate. Place salmon fillets crust side up on top of the vegetables. Garnish each fillet with 2 sprigs of mâche lettuce and serve immediately.

MATCHSTICK VEGETABLES

1 small carrot, peeled
1 stalk celery, tough strings
  removed
1 small red bell pepper, seeded and
  membranes removed
1 small yellow bell pepper, seeded
  and membranes removed
1 fennel bulb (use bulb part only)
1 small zucchini
1 small yellow squash
¹/₂ cup matchstick-sized julienne
  jicama
1 cup peanut oil
¹/₂ cup olive oil
¹/₂ cup white wine vinegar
2 tablespoons balsamic vinegar

2 shallots, finely chopped
2 cloves garlic, finely chopped
2 teaspoons finely chopped fresh
  basil
2 teaspoons finely chopped fresh
  parsley
2 teaspoons finely chopped fresh
  chives
2 teaspoons finely chopped fresh
  tarragon
2 teaspoons finely chopped fresh
  thyme
Salt to taste
Ground black pepper to taste
Juice of ¹/₂ lemon or to taste

Cut carrot, celery, peppers, and fennel into matchstick-sized julienne strips, making sure that pieces are of even size. Cut thick strips of peel off zucchini and yellow squash. Cut strips into matchstick julienne strips of even size.

Combine all julienne vegetables, including jicama, in a large bowl.

In a medium bowl, combine remaining ingredients and season to taste with salt, pepper, and lemon juice. Pour over julienne vegetables. Marinate for at least 10 minutes or up to several hours. Serve at room temperature and toss very well before serving, adjusting seasoning as needed.

Advance Preparation:

1. Four-peppercorn seasoning may be prepared several days in advance.
2. Matchstick Vegetables may be prepared and marinated several hours in advance. Serve at room temperature.

 WINE SUGGESTION:

CHARDONNAY, STAG'S LEAP WINE CELLARS, RESERVE, 1985
A crisp, clean, medium-bodied wine with green apple nose, with a hint of oak and good fruit flavors to contrast with the crunchy spice of the salmon.

Seared Salmon with Horseradish Potatoes and Hard-Boiled Egg–Caper Sauce

*Serves
6*

6 7-ounce pieces of salmon,
 trimmed of skin and bones
 Salt to taste
4 tablespoons peanut oil
 Horseradish Potatoes
 Caper Sauce
4 hard-boiled extra large egg whites,
 finely chopped
4 hard-boiled extra large egg yolks,
 finely chopped
1 cup fresh tomatoes, well drained,
 peeled, seeded, and cut into small
 dice (see page 271)

4 tablespoons whole capers
1½ teaspoons finely chopped fresh
 parsley
1½ teaspoons finely chopped fresh
 chives
1½ teaspoons finely chopped fresh
 basil
1½ teaspoons finely chopped fresh
 thyme

Place a large sauté pan over high heat. Season salmon on both sides with salt.

Add 2 tablespoons oil to the hot pan and heat to smoking. When pan is very hot, place 3 fillets in pan and sear for about 2 minutes to form a dark crust.

Turn each fillet and cook for about 2 minutes more, depending on the size and thickness of the fish. Salmon should be cooked medium-rare so that it is still slightly soft to the touch in the center.

Remove fillets from the pan and keep warm. Wipe the pan clean and repeat the process, using the remaining 2 tablespoons oil for the remaining 3 fillets. Keep warm.

Using a pastry bag with a large tip, pipe Horseradish Potatoes onto each of six warm dinner plates, forming a thick, straight line about 3½ inches long on one side of the plate. Or, more simply, spoon potatoes onto plates, mounding attractively in soft peaks on each side of the plate. Place a salmon fillet next to the potatoes so that the fish is in the middle of the plate. Ladle Caper Sauce around salmon and potatoes. Evenly sprinkle chopped egg whites and yolks, tomatoes, capers, and herbs over the sauce and serve immediately.

HORSERADISH POTATOES

2½ *pounds baking potatoes, peeled*
   and coarsely cubed
  5 *cups cold water*
   Salt to taste
  1 *cup heavy cream*
½ *cup loosely packed freshly grated*
   horseradish

2 *cloves garlic, finely minced*
1 *shallot, finely minced*
   Ground white pepper to taste
   Juice of 1 lemon
2 *tablespoons unsalted butter*

Place potatoes in a large saucepan with cold water and salt to taste. Bring to a boil. Reduce heat and simmer for about 30 minutes or until potatoes are very soft. Drain potatoes in a colander and place in a large mixer bowl.

Place cream in a small saucepan over medium heat. Add horseradish, garlic, and shallot. Bring cream to a boil, reduce heat, and simmer for 4 minutes.

Add hot horseradish cream to potatoes. Using an electric mixer, blend potatoes and cream until smooth. Season to taste with salt, white pepper, lemon juice, and butter. Remove potatoes from mixer bowl and keep warm.

CAPER SAUCE

1 *tablespoon peanut oil*
3 *white mushrooms, wiped clean*
   and thinly sliced
2 *shallots, peeled and chopped*
2 *sprigs fresh thyme*
2 *teaspoons cracked white*
   peppercorns
1 *tablespoon caper juice*

¼ *cup white wine*
 1 *tablespoon white wine vinegar*
½ *cup heavy cream*
 1 *cup very cold unsalted butter, cut*
   into small pieces
   Salt to taste
   Juice of ½ lemon or to taste

Heat oil in a medium saucepan over medium heat. Add mushrooms and sauté for 1 minute. Add shallots and sauté for another minute. Do not brown.

Add thyme, white peppercorns, caper juice, wine, and vinegar. Cook over high heat for about 8 minutes or until liquid has evaporated and ingredients are almost dry.

Add cream and cook over high heat for about 3 minutes or until reduced and thick.

Remove saucepan from heat and slowly whisk in butter piece by piece, forming an emulsion.

Strain sauce and season to taste with salt and lemon juice. Keep warm but do not let boil.

Advance Preparation:

1. Egg, tomato, caper, and herb garnishes may be prepared early in the day.
2. Potatoes may be prepared up to 2 hours in advance and kept warm.
3. Caper Sauce may be prepared up to 1 hour in advance and kept warm. If reheating, do not boil.

 WINE SUGGESTION:

PINOT GRIS, EYRIE VINEYARDS, 1985
A dry, medium-bodied wine with complex smoky bouquet and crisp fruit flavors provides contrast to the richness of the salmon and its sauce.

Halibut with Orange Horseradish Crust and Thai Shrimp Salad

*Serves
4*

Bob Zimmer's many years in the Orient inspired me to surprise him with a remembrance of the past. One of our room service captains, who is Thai, had introduced me to this Eastern technique for creating crunchy vegetables. I adapted it for use in this salad.

1 cup dry bread crumbs
2 tablespoons finely grated fresh
   horseradish
1½ tablespoons finely grated orange
   peel
1 clove garlic, minced
4 7-ounce halibut fillets, trimmed
   of skin, bones, and dark
   membrane

Salt to taste
3 tablespoons peanut oil
1 teaspoon sesame oil
   Thai Shrimp Salad

Preheat oven to 375°.

In a medium bowl, combine crumbs, horseradish, orange peel, and garlic. Spread mixture on a small plate or wax paper. Season halibut fillets lightly with salt, then press each fillet into crumb mixture, making sure both sides are completely covered.

Heat oils over medium heat in an ovenproof sauté pan large enough to hold fillets in a single layer.

Carefully place fillets in pan so as not to knock off crumbs. Cook 1 to 2 fillets at a time for easier handling. Cook for 1 to 2 minutes to brown crust, but *do not burn or blacken.*

When all fillets are brown on one side, arrange them, uncooked side down, in sauté pan and place in preheated 375° oven. Bake for about 5 minutes or just until fish is firm in the middle.

Place a halibut fillet on each of four warm dinner plates. Place Thai Shrimp Salad alongside fish, allowing 4 shrimp halves per serving. Dressing from salad should spread to cover the bottom of the plate. Add a bit more dressing if necessary, and serve immediately.

Warm Lobster Taco with Yellow Tomato Salsa and Jicama Salad (PAGE 5).

Tortilla Soup (PAGE 29).

Texas Black Bean and Jalapeño Jack Cheese Soups with Smoked Red and Yellow Pepper Creams (PAGE 36).

Crab Salad with Mexican Vegetables and Coriander-Cumin Vinaigrette (PAGE 57).

Clockwise from bottom left: Smoked Pheasant Salad with Ancho-Honey Vinaigrette and Spicy Fried Pasta (PAGE 64); *Grilled Swordfish with Pineapple–Red Chili Salsa* (PAGE 87); *The Mansion on Turtle Creek Breakfast Taco* (PAGE 215); *The Mansion on Turtle Creek Nachos* (PAGE 243).

Grilled Gulf Red Snapper with Tomatillo-Serrano Chili Vinaigrette and Corn-Bread Oysters (PAGE 75).

Oven-Baked Free-Range Chicken with Maple Pecan Crust and Pan Sauce, Roasted Garlic Potatoes, and Cranberry-Orange Relish in Sweet Potato Cups (PAGE 109).

Bottom, Medallions of Beef with Ancho Chili Sauce and Jicama–Black Bean Garnish (PAGE 129). *Top, Grilled Lamb Chops with Marjoram–Smoked Garlic Sauce and Barbecued Fire-Roasted Onions* (PAGE 141).

THAI SHRIMP SALAD

½ red bell pepper, seeded and
  membranes removed
½ yellow bell pepper, seeded and
  membranes removed
1 cup very thin vertical strips red
  onion
½ cup loosely packed whole fresh
  mint leaves, stems removed
½ cup loosely packed whole fresh
  cilantro leaves, stems removed
1 clove garlic, minced
1 shallot, minced

1½ tablespoons finely grated fresh
  ginger
1 serrano chili, seeded and minced
½ cup sweet rice wine vinegar
½ cup chicken stock (see page 262)
1 teaspoon sesame oil
1 teaspoon soy sauce
  Salt to taste
  Juice of 1 lime or to taste
1 tablespoon dark sesame oil
8 medium shrimp, peeled and
  deveined

Cut peppers vertically into thin strips. Place strips of onion, peppers, mint, and cilantro leaves in a large bowl with ice water to cover. This is very important because it ensures that vegetables will stay crisp.

In a small bowl, combine garlic, shallot, ginger, serrano chili, vinegar, chicken stock, sesame oil, and soy sauce, whisking to blend. Season to taste with salt and lime juice. Cover and set aside.

Heat dark sesame oil in a large sauté pan over medium-high heat. Add shrimp and lightly season to taste with salt. Stir-fry shrimp just until firm and no longer translucent. Remove from pan, slice in half lengthwise, and keep warm.

Drain vegetables and herbs, making sure all excess moisture is removed. Place in a large bowl. Gather ends together loosely and gently twirl several times, being careful not to crush leaves.

Add shrimp and pour dressing over. Toss lightly to combine and coat ingredients with dressing. This salad must be assembled at the last moment to retain the crispness of the iced vegetables and herbs.

Advance Preparation:

1. Salad dressing may be mixed several hours ahead.
2. Vegetables may be cut and iced 1 hour before serving.

 WINE SUGGESTION:

GEWURZTRAMINER, CLOS DU BOIS, EARLY HARVEST, 1985
A spicy, medium-dry wine with a tart apricot taste and orange blossom nose works well with the citrus and Oriental flavors of this dish.

HALIBUT BREADED WITH CASHEWS SERVED WITH MANGO-BASIL SAUCE

*Serves
4*

I have won many fish cooking contests with this recipe—it is Dallasites' favorite fish dish. The Mango-Basil Sauce has no cream or butter—just the great flavor of mango to make it a low-calorie dream!

*¹/₄ pound unsalted cashews, roasted
   and ground medium-fine*
¹/₂ cup dry fine bread crumbs
 *4 6-ounce pieces halibut (or any
   white fish), trimmed of skin and
   bones*

Salt to taste
3 to 4 tablespoons peanut oil
Mango-Basil Sauce

Preheat oven to 375°.

Combine ground cashews and bread crumbs, and spread on a small plate or wax paper. Season halibut with salt to taste and press into crumb mixture until completely coated.

Heat oil in an ovenproof sauté pan over medium heat. Carefully place breaded halibut in pan and cook until lightly browned on one side. Do not burn or blacken. Turn and place pan in preheated 375° oven. Bake for about 5 minutes or until fish is firm. Do not overcook.

Place 1 breaded halibut piece in the middle of each of four warm dinner plates. Surround with Mango-Basil Sauce and serve immediately.

MANGO-BASIL SAUCE

3 very large ripe mangoes, peeled,
   seeded, and coarsely chopped
2 tablespoons grated fresh ginger
3 cups chicken stock (see page 262)
5 medium fresh basil leaves, rinsed
   and dried

Salt to taste
Juice of 1 lime or to taste
Pure maple syrup, to taste, if needed

Combine mangoes, ginger, and chicken stock in a large saucepan. Bring to a boil, reduce heat, and simmer for about 20 minutes or until liquid is reduced by half.

Pour mixture into a blender or food processor and blend until very smooth. Place basil leaves in mango sauce and pour into top half of a double boiler over hot water. Let steep for at least 20 min-utes. Just before serving, remove basil leaves and season to taste with salt and lime juice. If added sweetness is desired, add pure maple syrup to taste.

Advance Preparation:
1. Mango-Basil Sauce may be prepared a few hours before serving and kept warm.

 WINE SUGGESTION:

CHARDONNAY, SAINTSBURY, 1985
Crisp, dry, medium-bodied wine with oak overtones but balanced fruit flavors works well with the combination of nuts and fruit in this dish.

GRILLED REDFISH WITH ARTICHOKE-OYSTER SAUCE AND CRISP SHOESTRING YAMS

*Serves
4*

4 *7-ounce redfish fillets, trimmed of
   skin, bones, and dark membrane*
2 *tablespoons peanut oil
   Salt to taste
   The Mansion on Turtle Creek Pepper
   Mixture to taste (see page 261)*

*Artichoke-Oyster Sauce
Crisp Shoestring Yams*

Preheat grill or light coals (see page 275). Make sure grates are clean, and lightly rub or brush with oil just before placing fish on grill.

Brush fillets with 2 tablespoons peanut oil and season to taste with salt and Pepper Mixture.

Place fillets on grill and cook for about 2 minutes or just long enough to mark one side. Turn and cook for about 2 minutes more or just until fish flakes, depending on the size and thickness of fillets. Allow about 4 minutes cooking time for each ½ inch of thickness at the thickest part. Do not overcook. The fish should be very moist.

Ladle enough Artichoke-Oyster Sauce onto each of four warm dinner plates to cover the bottom of the plate. Place a redfish fillet in the middle of each plate and put 2 artichoke leaves overlapping each other on either side of each fillet (total of 4 leaves to a plate), with tip ends pointing toward rim of plate. Place a small mound of Crisp Shoestring Yams at the base of each artichoke grouping next to the fish and serve immediately.

ARTICHOKE-OYSTER SAUCE

2 *large artichokes, stems attached*
1 *tablespoon peanut oil*
2 *large white mushrooms, rubbed*
    clean and sliced thin
1 *shallot, peeled and chopped*
1 *clove garlic, chopped*
1 *serrano chili, seeded and chopped*

2 *sprigs fresh thyme*
1 *cup chicken stock (see page 262)*
1 *cup heavy cream*
3 *medium leaves fresh spinach*
5 *fresh oysters, shucked and drained*
    Salt to taste
    Juice of ½ lemon or to taste

Using scissors, trim sharp ends of artichoke leaves. Place artichokes in a large pot and cover with water. Cover pot and bring water to a boil. Cook for 45 minutes or until leaves and stem end are tender when fork is inserted.

Drain artichokes and cool. When artichokes are cool enough to handle, carefully pull out 16 large green leaves. Trim neatly and reserve for garnish. Remove the remaining leaves and choke and discard, reserving the artichoke bottoms for sauce.

Heat oil in a large saucepan over medium heat. When oil is hot, add mushrooms and sauté for 1 minute. Add shallot, garlic, and serrano chili and sauté for 1 minute.

Add thyme, chicken stock, and cream. Bring to a boil and cook for about 8 minutes or until reduced by one-third. Add artichoke bottoms. Pour mixture, including artichoke bottoms, into a blender or food processor, along with spinach leaves.

Process until smooth, in several batches if necessary to accommodate size of container.

While blender or processor is still running, add oysters one by one. Process until all ingredients are puréed.

Strain and season to taste with salt and lemon juice. If sauce is too thick, thin with chicken stock. Keep warm.

CRISP SHOESTRING YAMS

4 cups peanut oil
½ large yam or sweet potato, peeled

Salt to taste

Heat oil in a deep pot with high sides or a deep-fat fryer to 375°.

Slice yam ⅛ inch thick and cut into a very fine julienne, as for shoestring potatoes.

Drop julienne yam in small batches into hot oil and fry for 2 minutes. Stir to ensure even cooking and to separate strands. Do not burn.

Remove yam from hot oil with a slotted spoon and drain on paper towel. When all shoestring yams have been fried and drained, bring oil to 390°.

Return shoestrings to oil and cook for an additional 1 to 2 minutes or until crisp. Remove from oil and drain on paper towel. Lightly sprinkle with salt to taste. Keep warm until all shoestring yams are fried.

Advance Preparation:
1. Sauce may be prepared up to 1 hour in advance and kept warm.
2. Yams may be deep-fried just before cooking redfish and kept warm.

 WINE SUGGESTION:

CHARDONNAY, FLORA SPRINGS, BARREL FERMENTED, 1984
A rich, full-bodied wine with oaky, butter nose and enough acidity and texture in taste to complement the intense flavors of the artichoke sauce and its interplay with the grilled fish.

SOLE FILLETS WITH MACADAMIA NUT CRUST
WITH PAPAYA-BASIL SAUCE

*Serves
4*

³/4 *cup finely ground toasted bread
    crumbs*
¹/4 *cup macadamia nuts, finely
    ground (be sure all salt is
    removed)*

4 *6-ounce sole fillets, trimmed of
    skin and bones
    Salt to taste*
3 *to 4 tablespoons peanut oil
    Papaya-Basil Sauce*

Preheat oven to 400°.

Combine bread crumbs and macadamia nuts, and spread on a small plate or wax paper. Season sole with salt to taste and press fillets into crumb mixture to coat all sides.

Heat oil in a large ovenproof sauté pan over medium heat. Carefully place breaded sole in sauté pan and cook for about 1 to 2 minutes or until lightly brown on one side.

Turn fillets. Place sauté pan in preheated 400° oven and bake for 5 minutes or just until fish flakes.

Place one sole fillet in the center of each of four warm dinner plates. Spoon Papaya-Basil Sauce around the fish and serve immediately.

PAPAYA-BASIL SAUCE

1¹/2 *cups fresh papaya pulp*
  1 *teaspoon vegetable oil*
  1 *large shallot, minced*
¹/4 *cup dry white wine*
  2 *sprigs fresh thyme*

1¹/4 *cups chicken stock (see page 262)*
1¹/2 *cups heavy cream*
  5 *fresh basil leaves*
    Salt to taste

Blend papaya pulp thoroughly in a food processor or blender and set aside.

Heat oil in a medium saucepan and add shallot. Cook, stirring frequently, about 1 minute.

Add wine and thyme and cook until

the wine evaporates. Add 1 cup chicken stock, bring to a boil, reduce heat, and simmer for about 10 minutes or until reduced by half.

Add cream and boil over relatively high heat for about 8 minutes or until reduced to approximately 1½ cups.

Add papaya pulp, remaining ¼ cup chicken stock, basil leaves, and salt to cream sauce. Pour into a small saucepan and cook for 10 minutes.

Pour sauce through a fine sieve and press the solids against sides with a wooden spoon or spatula to extract as much liquid as possible.

Allow basil leaves to steep in sauce for about 20 minutes. Just before serving, remove basil leaves from sauce, adjust seasoning, and serve. If necessary, add a little chicken stock to thin the sauce to the desired consistency.

Advance Preparation:
1. Sauce may be prepared up to 1 day ahead and refrigerated. Reheat and adjust for consistency, and taste just before serving.

 WINE SUGGESTION:

SPARKLING WINE, GLORIA FERRER, NATURAL SONOMA CUVÉE EMERALD, N.V.
Bone-dry wine with slightly smoky bouquet and clean, crisp citrus taste to provide contrast to the buttery macadamias and spicy fruit sauce.

Poultry

GRILLED FREE-RANGE CHICKEN WITH SMOKED PEPPER BUTTER
AND TOBACCO ONIONS

OVEN-BAKED FREE-RANGE CHICKEN WITH MAPLE PECAN CRUST
AND PAN SAUCE, ROASTED GARLIC POTATOES, AND CRANBERRY-ORANGE
RELISH IN SWEET POTATO CUPS

GRILLED SPRING CHICKEN WITH A SPICY RED ONION—POBLANO
CHILI RELISH, TWO SAUCES OF SMOKED RED AND ROASTED
YELLOW BELL PEPPERS, AND GRANNY FEARING'S KENTUCKY BAKED BEANS

GRILLED CHICKEN BREASTS WITH WARM CUCUMBER SALAD
AND ARTICHOKE-LIME SAUCE

GRILLED FREE-RANGE CHICKEN
WITH SMOKED PEPPER BUTTER AND TOBACCO ONIONS

Serves
6

3 *small free-range chickens or small*
   (2-pound) fryers
Salt to taste
The Mansion on Turtle Creek Pepper
Mixture to taste (see page 261)

Tobacco Onions
Smoked Pepper Butter

Ask butcher to halve chickens, remove wings, and debone except for drumsticks.

Preheat grill.

Generously season chicken halves with salt and Pepper Mixture. Make sure grates are clean, and lightly rub or brush with oil. Place chicken halves on preheated grill, skin side down. Cook for about 7 minutes or until skin is golden brown and crisp. Turn halves and cook for about 6 minutes or until meat is no longer pink and thigh juices run clear.

Place Tobacco Onions in the middle of each of six warm dinner plates, creating a "bird's nest." Nestle a chicken half on top of onions on each plate so onions surround the bird. Place 3 rounds of Smoked Pepper Butter on top of each bird and serve immediately while butter is melting.

TOBACCO ONIONS

5 *cups peanut oil*
3 *cups flour*
1½ *teaspoons cayenne pepper*
1 *tablespoon paprika*
  Salt to taste

Ground black pepper to taste
1 *large Spanish onion, peeled and*
  sliced into very thin rings
1 *red onion, peeled and sliced into*
  very thin rings

Heat oil in a deep saucepan to 350°.

In a large mixing bowl, blend flour, cayenne, paprika, salt, and pepper. Separate onion rings and dredge in the flour mixture, shaking off excess flour.

Carefully place onion rings in the hot

oil in small batches, making sure rings don't stick together. Fry for 3 to 5 minutes or until golden brown. Remove with a slotted spoon, drain briefly on paper towel, and place on a warm platter. Repeat until all onions are fried. Keep warm.

SMOKED PEPPER BUTTER

½ *small red bell pepper*
½ *small yellow bell pepper*
1 *large clove garlic, finely chopped*
1 *shallot, finely chopped*
½ *tablespoon Dijon mustard*
½ *tablespoon fresh cilantro leaves, finely chopped, stems removed*

1 *serrano chili, seeded and finely chopped*
1 *tablespoon lime juice*
2 *teaspoons lemon juice*
½ *cup softened unsalted butter*
  Salt to taste
  Ground black pepper to taste

Cut peppers in half and remove seeds. Cut away internal membrane and smoke halves for 15 to 20 minutes (see page 272). When smoked, cut into small dice (see page 271) and set aside.

Combine garlic, shallot, mustard, cilantro, serrano chili, lime and lemon juices, and butter in the work bowl of a food processor. Process, using the steel blade, until smooth. Add salt and pepper to taste. Remove blade, and with a rubber spatula, blend in diced smoked peppers. Do not process; diced pepper should be visible in butter.

Place butter on a long sheet of wax paper to form a cylinder about 1½ inches in diameter. Roll the paper around the butter and twist each end to seal. Place roll in refrigerator for about 2 hours or until solid.

When ready to use, unroll wax paper and cut butter into 18 ¼-inch-thick rounds.

Advance Preparation:
1. Butter must be prepared at least 2 hours in advance and may be prepared up to several days ahead and refrigerated.
2. Onions may be fried up to 1 hour before serving and kept warm.

WINE SUGGESTION:

BLANC DE PINOT NOIR, BUENA VISTA STEELHEAD RUN, 1985
An off-dry, medium-bodied rosé with a berry nose and fresh, full-bodied, fruity taste to play against the smoky, spicy flavors of this dish.

Oven-Baked Free-Range Chicken with Maple Pecan Crust and Pan Sauce, Roasted Garlic Potatoes, and Cranberry-Orange Relish in Sweet Potato Cups

Serves
4

When I first proposed this dish for the menu, everyone thought it was too "homey" for the sophisticated dining we offer at The Mansion on Turtle Creek. I wanted to give our patrons something familiar yet update it to fit in with our menu. Bob Zimmer and I, after many discussions, decided to include it, and it is now one of our most popular entrées.

2 3-pound free-range chickens or
  fryers
Salt to taste
The Mansion on Turtle Creek
Pepper Mixture to taste (see page
261)
2 tablespoons vegetable oil
1 cup finely ground pecans
1 tablespoon Dijon mustard
1 tablespoon pure maple syrup

1 tablespoon reserved chicken
  grease
1 lightly beaten egg white
2 tablespoons brandy
1¹/₂ cups brown veal demi-glace (see
  page 263)
  Roasted Garlic Potatoes
  Cranberry-Orange Relish in Sweet
  Potato Cups

Preheat oven to 400°.

Remove wings from chickens. Starting at keel bone, run the tip of a knife between breast meat and bone back to the thigh so that boneless breast and thigh meat separate in one piece. Leave skin on. Cutting from underside, re-move thigh and leg bones. Repeat for other bird so that you have 4 boneless half chickens.

Season chickens with salt and Pepper Mixture. Heat oil in an ovenproof sauté pan large enough to hold chicken halves in a single layer. Sauté chicken, skin side down, for about 5 minutes or until a light brown crust has formed, being careful not to burn.

Turn halves skin side up and place sauté pan in preheated 400° oven. Roast the birds for 8 minutes, then remove from oven. Pour off grease, reserving 1 tablespoon.

Combine pecans, mustard, maple syrup, reserved chicken grease, egg white, and salt to taste.

Spoon mixture over each bird. Using the back of a spoon, cover skin with a thin coating. Return pan to oven for about 8 minutes or until chicken is crispy and juices run clear.

Remove from oven. Place chicken on a warm platter. Pour excess fat from sauté pan. Over high heat, deglaze pan with brandy. Cook just until aroma of alcohol burns off. Stir in demi-glace. Reduce heat and simmer for 5 minutes.

Cover the bottom of each of four hot dinner plates with pan sauce. Carefully place one chicken half on each. Do not break crust.

Using a pastry bag with a large star tip, pipe 2 swirls of Roasted Garlic Potatoes on each side of the chicken, forming small mounds. (If pastry bag is not available, make small mounds with a rounded tablespoon.) Garnish the plates with Cranberry-Orange Relish in Sweet Potato Cups. Serve immediately.

ROASTED GARLIC POTATOES

*2 pounds baking potatoes, peeled
    and cubed
1 tablespoon peanut oil
8 whole cloves garlic, peeled
    Leaves from 1 small bunch fresh
    thyme (3 or 4 sprigs), minced*

*1/4 cup heavy cream
    Juice of 1 lemon
3 tablespoons unsalted butter
    Salt to taste*

Preheat oven to 350°.

In a medium saucepan, cover potatoes with cold water and bring to a boil. Cook for about 20 minutes or until soft. Drain and place in large bowl of an electric mixer.

In a small ovenproof sauté pan, heat oil and lightly brown whole garlic cloves over medium heat. Place pan with garlic in preheated 350° oven and roast for about 12 minutes or until garlic is soft. Turn garlic occasionally and do not burn.

Place garlic in a blender or food processor with thyme, cream, and lemon juice. Blend until smooth.

Beat potatoes with electric mixer. Add roasted garlic mixture and beat until smooth. Add butter and season to taste with salt. Keep warm.

CRANBERRY-ORANGE RELISH IN SWEET POTATO CUPS

1 cup cranberries
   Zest and sections of 1 orange, pith
   removed and seeded
   Zest of 1 small lemon
2 teaspoons grated fresh ginger
2 teaspoons chopped fresh cilantro

Pure maple syrup to taste
5 cups peanut oil
4 very thin raw sweet potato rounds,
   about 3 inches in diameter
4 small fresh mint leaves

Using fine die of a food grinder, grind cranberries, orange zest and sections, lemon zest, ginger, and cilantro into a small bowl (or process finely in a food processor). Add maple syrup to taste and mix well. Cover and set aside.

Preheat oil to 350° in a small deep fryer. Fit a sweet potato round into a 2-ounce ladle. Insert a 1-ounce ladle into the 2-ounce ladle so the sweet potato forms a cup shape. Submerge both ladles in hot oil and cook sweet potato for about 1 minute. Do not brown. Remove from oil. Carefully separate the 1-ounce ladle from the larger one and remove sweet potato cup onto paper towel to drain. Repeat to make 4 cups.

Fill each cup with cranberry-orange relish and place a mint leaf on top.

Advance Preparation:
1. Relish may be prepared up to 1 day ahead and refrigerated, tightly covered. Serve at room temperature.
2. Potatoes may be prepared up to 1 hour before serving and kept warm.
3. Sweet potato cups may be fried just before roasting chicken.

 WINE SUGGESTION:

JOHANNISBERG RIESLING, FETZER, 1985
Fresh, off-dry wine with spicy floral nose and a fruity taste with good acidity to complement the sweetish maple crust and the slightly tart relish.

GRILLED SPRING CHICKEN
WITH A SPICY RED ONION–POBLANO CHILI RELISH,
TWO SAUCES OF SMOKED RED AND ROASTED YELLOW
BELL PEPPERS, AND GRANNY FEARING'S
KENTUCKY BAKED BEANS

Serves
6

The flavor of these baked beans has always been a part of my life. My grandmother always prepared them for large family gatherings on Sundays and holidays. I think they taste particularly good with grilled chicken.

3 spring chickens or very small
  fryers, split in half, wing tips
  removed
Salt to taste
The Mansion on Turtle Creek
  Pepper Mixture to taste (see page
  261)
⅛ cup olive oil
⅛ cup peanut oil

Juice of 1 lime
Juice of 1 lemon
Smoked Red Bell Pepper Sauce
Roasted Yellow Bell Pepper Sauce
Spicy Red Onion–Poblano Chili
  Relish
Granny Fearing's Kentucky Baked
  Beans

Preheat grill. Season chickens on all sides with salt and Pepper Mixture to taste. Combine olive and peanut oils and brush liberally on the chickens. Place on grill over coals. Baste occasionally with any remaining oil while cooking.

Grill for about 25 minutes or until skin is golden and juices in leg and thigh run clear.

Combine lime and lemon juices and brush on chickens after grilling. Keep warm.

Cover the bottom of each of six warm dinner plates with sauces: half of plate with Smoked Red Bell Pepper Sauce and the other half with Roasted Yellow Bell Pepper Sauce. Place 1 chicken half in the middle and a small mound of Spicy Red Onion–Poblano Chili Relish on either side of chicken, and serve immediately with Granny Fearing's Kentucky Baked Beans.

SMOKED RED BELL PEPPER SAUCE

2 red bell peppers
2 teaspoons peanut oil
2 tablespoons finely chopped onion
2 sprigs fresh thyme
³/₄ cup chicken stock (see page 262)

³/₄ cup heavy cream
1 clove garlic, peeled
 Salt to taste
 Juice of ¹/₂ lemon or to taste

Smoke peppers for 20 minutes (see page 272). Remove stem, seeds, and inner membranes. Cut into small pieces and set aside.

Heat oil in a medium saucepan over medium heat. Add onion and sauté for about 5 minutes or until transparent.

Add thyme and chicken stock. Bring liquid to a boil, lower heat, and cook until liquid is reduced by half.

Add cream and boil hard for 3 minutes. Remove from heat and remove thyme.

In a blender or food processor, combine smoked pepper, cream mixture, and garlic clove. Process until smooth. Season to taste with salt and lemon juice. Keep warm.

ROASTED YELLOW BELL PEPPER SAUCE

2 yellow bell peppers
2 teaspoons peanut oil
2 tablespoons finely chopped onion
2 sprigs fresh thyme
³/₄ cup chicken stock (see page 262)

³/₄ cup heavy cream
1 clove garlic, peeled
 Salt to taste
 Juice of ¹/₂ lemon or to taste

Roast peppers over flame or under broiler until charred on all sides. Pull charred skin from pepper and remove stem, seeds, and inner membranes. Cut into small pieces and set aside.

Heat oil in a medium saucepan over medium heat. Add onion and sauté for about 5 minutes or until transparent.

Add thyme and chicken stock. Bring liquid to a boil, lower heat, and cook until liquid is reduced by half.

Add cream and boil hard for 3 minutes. Remove from heat and remove thyme.

In a blender or food processor, combine roasted pepper, cream mixture, and garlic clove. Process until smooth. Season to taste with salt and lemon juice. Keep warm.

SPICY RED ONION—POBLANO CHILI RELISH

1½ tablespoons olive oil
1 medium red onion, cut into
   medium dice (see page 271)
1½ medium poblano chilies, charred,
   peeled, seeded, and cut into
   medium dice (see page 271)
1 large clove garlic, minced
½ tablespoon finely chopped fresh
   mint

½ tablespoon finely chopped green
   onion
1 tablespoon balsamic vinegar
½ tablespoon white wine
Juice of 1 lime
Salt to taste

Heat oil in a large sauté pan over medium heat. Sauté onion for about 5 minutes or until soft but not mushy.

Place onion in a medium bowl and add remaining ingredients. Toss and marinate relish for at least 20 minutes. Serve at room temperature.

GRANNY FEARING'S KENTUCKY BAKED BEANS

1 21-ounce can pork and beans
1 large onion, finely chopped
1 12-ounce bottle Heinz ketchup
1 tablespoon yellow mustard
1⅛ cups packed light brown sugar
⅛ cup molasses

⅛ cup Heinz sweet gherkin juice
1 teaspoon apple cider vinegar
Salt to taste
Ground black pepper to taste
½ pound thickly sliced smoked
   bacon

Preheat oven to 350°.

Combine pork and beans, onion, ketchup, mustard, brown sugar, molasses, gherkin juice, vinegar, salt, and pepper to taste in a 2-quart casserole. Top with strips of bacon in a crisscross pattern. Cover with aluminum foil. Bake in preheated 350° oven for 1½

hours. Remove foil for last 30 minutes of baking. Serve hot or cold.

Advance Preparation:

1. Relish may be prepared up to 1 day ahead and refrigerated. Allow to warm to room temperature before serving.

2. Sauces may be prepared up to 1 day ahead and refrigerated. Reheat gently.

3. Beans may be prepared up to 1 day ahead and refrigerated. Warm in 350° oven for no more than 20 minutes.

4. Chickens may be grilled up to 1 hour before serving and kept warm.

 WINE SUGGESTION:

FUMÉ BLANC, DE LOACH, 1985

Dry, medium-bodied wine with a spicy herbal nose and full-flavored finish with good acidity to complement the peppers of the sauce and accommodate the spicy relish.

Grilled Chicken Breasts with Warm Cucumber Salad and Artichoke-Lime Sauce

*Serves
4*

4 boneless, skinless chicken breast
   halves
2 tablespoons peanut oil
   Salt to taste

Ground black pepper to taste
Artichoke-Lime Sauce
Warm Cucumber Salad
8 to 12 reserved artichoke leaves

Preheat grill. Make sure grates are clean, and lightly rub or brush with oil. Brush chicken breasts with 2 tablespoons peanut oil and season to taste with salt and pepper. Place on grill and cook for 5 minutes. Turn and cook for about 3 minutes more or until juices run clear.

Ladle Artichoke-Lime Sauce over the bottom of each of four warm dinner plates. In the middle of the plate, place a portion of Warm Cucumber Salad to make a "bird's nest." Arrange a grilled chicken breast on top and garnish with 2 or 3 artichoke leaves. Serve immediately.

WARM CUCUMBER SALAD

2 small cucumbers, peeled and
   seeded
2 quarts ice water
1 tablespoon sesame oil

2 tablespoons peanut oil
1 tablespoon tarragon vinegar
   Salt to taste

One day in advance, cut cucumbers into 1½-inch pieces. Slice pieces lengthwise into strips as thin as possible. Refrigerate in ice water overnight to crisp. Slices should be translucent, as for pickling. Hold in ice water until just

before serving. Add more ice as needed if cubes melt. Drain cucumbers and place on paper towel to eliminate excess moisture.

Mix oils and vinegar. Season to taste with salt and set aside.

Sauté cucumbers in a dry, hot sauté pan, turning constantly to keep them from browning, for about 2 minutes or until heated through. When cucumbers are hot, drain off any liquid and toss cucumbers with the oil mixture. Serve immediately.

Advance Preparation:
1. Peel, seed, and slice cucumbers and store in ice water overnight to crisp.
2. Sauce may be prepared several hours in advance and kept warm. Whisk in butter just before serving.

ARTICHOKE-LIME SAUCE

8 *small (or 4 large) artichokes, washed and trimmed*
1 *cup chicken stock (see page 262)*
2 *cups heavy cream*

Juice of 2 limes
Salt to taste
2 *tablespoons unsalted butter*

Steam artichokes for 40 minutes or until tender. Immerse in ice water to cool. Remove leaves and choke, reserving the bottoms. Reserve 8 to 12 unblemished leaves for garnish.

In a large saucepan, bring chicken stock to a boil and cook for about 15 minutes or until liquid is reduced by half. Add cream; bring to a boil. Lower heat slightly and cook for about 8 minutes or until liquid is reduced and thick enough to coat the back of a spoon lightly.

Combine artichoke bottoms with the reduced stock mixture in a food processor or blender and process until smooth. Add lime juice and salt to taste. Keep warm. Just before serving, whisk in butter.

 WINE SUGGESTION:

SAUVIGNON BLANC, PRESTON, CUVÉE DE FUMÉ, 1985
Dry, medium-bodied wine with a slightly herbal nose and crisp fruit flavors with hints of lemon and wood that will accommodate the acids of this dish and enhance the grilled flavor of the chicken.

Veal

MEDALLIONS OF VEAL WITH AGED WHITE CHEDDAR—
WILD MUSHROOM SAUCE SERVED WITH ASPARAGUS-LEEK COMPOTE

PAN-SEARED VEAL CHOP WITH SAUCE OF TANGERINES,
SMOKED PEPPERS, WILD RICE, AND MARIGOLD MINT AND JICAMA COMPOTE

MEDALLIONS OF VEAL WITH AGED WHITE CHEDDAR–
WILD MUSHROOM SAUCE SERVED WITH ASPARAGUS-LEEK COMPOTE

Serves
4

4 tablespoons peanut oil
8 2½-ounce veal loin fillets, about ½
  inch thick
  Salt to taste

Aged White Cheddar–Wild Mushroom Sauce
Asparagus-Leek Compote

Heat oil in a large sauté pan over medium heat. Season fillets with salt to taste and quickly sauté veal for about 3 minutes on one side. Turn medallions and brown for 2 minutes. Do not crowd pan. Remove from pan and keep warm.

Ladle Aged White Cheddar–Wild Mushroom Sauce over the bottom of each of four warm dinner plates. Place 2 medallions of veal on each plate. Garnish with equal portions of Asparagus-Leek Compote and serve immediately.

AGED WHITE CHEDDAR–WILD MUSHROOM SAUCE

½ pound veal bones, cut into small
  pieces
1 tablespoon peanut oil
2 large white mushrooms, wiped
  clean and sliced thin
2 large shallots, peeled and chopped
1 clove garlic, peeled and chopped
2 sprigs fresh thyme
2 cups chicken stock (see page 262)
1 cup heavy cream

½ cup grated aged white cheddar
  cheese
1 tablespoon unsalted butter
1½ cups assorted wild mushrooms
  (such as shiitake, chanterelles,
  pleurotes) sliced in thin julienne
  strips
  Salt to taste
  Juice of ½ lemon or to taste

Preheat oven to 400°.
   Ask butcher to cut veal bones into pieces. Place bones on a baking sheet and place in preheated 400° oven. Roast for about 12 to 15 minutes or until

brown. Be careful not to burn or blacken.
   Heat oil in a large saucepan over medium heat. Add white mushrooms and sauté for 1 minute. Add shallots and

garlic; sauté for 1 minute. Add browned veal bones, thyme, and chicken stock. Bring to a boil, lower heat, and simmer for 20 minutes.

Add cream and return liquid to a boil. Lower heat and simmer for about 15 minutes or until liquid is reduced by about one-quarter or thick enough to coat the back of a spoon. Remove bones from sauce. Pour sauce into a food pro-cessor or blender along with cheese. Process until smooth. Strain and keep warm.

Place a medium sauté pan over medium heat. Melt butter, then add wild mushrooms. Sauté mushrooms for 2 minutes. Season lightly with salt. Fold cooked mushrooms into sauce. Adjust seasoning with salt and lemon juice.

ASPARAGUS-LEEK COMPOTE

¼ pound green asparagus, washed and trimmed
1 medium leek, white part only
¼ pound smoked bacon

1 tablespoon butter
2 ripe tomatoes, peeled, seeded, and cut into ½-inch dice (see page 271)
Salt to taste

Place a large pot of water over high heat and bring to a boil.

Plunge asparagus in boiling water and cook for about 3 minutes. Remove and place in a colander. Rinse with cold water to stop cooking. Drain well and cut diagonally into ¾-inch pieces.

Clean leek well, being careful to remove all sand. Cut leek into 4 pieces lengthwise. Cut long pieces diagonally into ¾-inch pieces. Plunge leek pieces in boiling water and cook for about 2 minutes. Remove and place in a colander. Rinse with cold water to stop the cooking. Drain well.

Cut bacon into ½-inch dice (see page 271). Sauté, over medium heat, until brown. Drain on paper towel.

Melt butter in a small saucepan over medium heat. When butter begins to foam, add asparagus, leek, tomatoes, and bacon. Sauté for 3 minutes. Season to taste with salt and serve immediately.

Advance Preparation:
1. Sauce may be prepared up to 3 hours ahead and kept warm.
2. Vegetables and bacon for compote may be prepared up to 3 hours ahead, but compote cannot be put together until the last minute.

 WINE SUGGESTION:

CHARDONNAY, LEEWARD, MACGREGOR VINEYARDS, 1984
A rich, full-bodied wine with a toasty nose and complex fruit and oak flavors to complement the elegant combination of wild mushrooms and aged cheese.

PAN-SEARED VEAL CHOP WITH SAUCE OF TANGERINES, SMOKED PEPPERS, WILD RICE, AND MARIGOLD MINT AND JICAMA COMPOTE

Serves
4

The beautiful tangerine base of this sauce combined with the colors of the garnishes presents a flavor of Santa Fe—the pattern of an Indian blanket sits before the diner.

4 9- to 10-ounce veal chops, bone in,
    trimmed of fat
    Salt to taste
1 *tablespoon vegetable oil*

Sauce of Tangerines, Smoked Peppers, Wild Rice, and Marigold Mint
Jicama Compote

Preheat oven to 400°.

Season chops with salt to taste. Heat oil in a large ovenproof sauté pan over medium heat. Place chops in hot pan and sear for 5 minutes to form a heavy brown crust, being careful not to burn edges.

Turn chops and place sauté pan in preheated 400° oven for 10 minutes to finish cooking.

Ladle Sauce of Tangerines, Smoked Peppers, Wild Rice, and Marigold Mint over the bottom of each of four warm dinner plates. Place a veal chop in the middle of each plate. Spoon a small amount of Jicama Compote on the bone side of each chop. Serve immediately.

SAUCE OF TANGERINES, SMOKED PEPPERS, WILD RICE, AND MARIGOLD MINT

1 tablespoon diced red bell pepper (see page 271)
1 tablespoon diced yellow bell pepper (see page 271)
1 tablespoon diced green bell pepper (see page 271)
1/2 pound veal bones, broken into small pieces
1 teaspoon vegetable oil
2 shallots, chopped
1 clove garlic, chopped
1 serrano chili, seeded and chopped
1 1/2 cups tangerine juice

1/2 cup chicken stock (see page 262)
1/4 cup brown veal demi-glace (see page 263)
4 tablespoons cold unsalted butter, cut into small pieces
1/3 cup cooked wild rice
1 tablespoon minced marigold mint (if unavailable, substitute 2 teaspoons minced fresh mint and 1 teaspoon fresh tarragon)
Salt to taste
Juice of 1/2 lime or to taste

Smoke peppers for 15 minutes (see page 272). Set aside.

Preheat oven to 400°.

Place veal bones in a single layer in a shallow baking pan and roast in preheated 400° oven for about 10 minutes or until light brown.

Heat oil in a large saucepan over medium heat. Add shallots, garlic, and serrano chili and sauté for 1 minute. Add tangerine juice, chicken stock, and bones. Bring to a boil. Lower heat and simmer for 20 minutes.

Strain mixture into a medium saucepan. Bring to a boil, add demi-glace, and cook for about 8 minutes or until liquid is reduced and thick enough to coat the back of a spoon. Remove from heat and slowly whisk in butter one piece at a time; strain. Fold peppers, wild rice, and marigold mint into sauce. Stir in salt and lime juice to taste. Keep warm but *do not allow sauce to boil* or it will separate.

JICAMA COMPOTE

1 cup finely diced jicama (see page 271)
1/4 cup heavy cream

Salt to taste
Juice of 1/2 lime or to taste
Cayenne pepper to taste

Place jicama and cream in a small saucepan over medium heat. Bring liq-

uid to a boil, reduce heat, and cook for about 5 minutes or until cream has thickened enough to coat jicama thoroughly.

Season to taste with salt, lime juice, and cayenne pepper. Keep warm.

Advance Preparation:

1. Compote may be prepared up to 2 hours ahead. Keep warm or gently reheat before serving.

2. Sauce may be prepared up to 2 hours ahead and kept warm. Reheat very gently, if necessary, so sauce does not curdle.

3. Chops may be seared and roasted up to 30 minutes ahead and kept warm.

 WINE SUGGESTION:

CABERNET SAUVIGNON, SILVERADO, 1983
Deep, subtle wine with currant, mint nose, and balanced oak and fruit flavors to complement the minted spicy sauce with the veal.

Beef

MEDALLIONS OF BEEF WITH ANCHO CHILI SAUCE
AND JICAMA—BLACK BEAN GARNISH

MARINATED GRILLED TENDERLOIN OF BEEF
WITH TOMATILLO—SERRANO CHILI SAUCE AND SMOKED
CORN CAKES

GRILLED SIRLOIN STEAK WITH BLACK BEAN "CHILI" SAUCE

MEDALLIONS OF BEEF WITH ANCHO CHILI SAUCE AND JICAMA–BLACK BEAN GARNISH

*Serves
4*

*My good friend Stephan Pyles, my in-town rival, introduced me
to a similar sauce at his restaurant Routh Street Café. The com-
petition between us keeps us honest!*

8 3-ounce beef tenderloin fillets,
  trimmed of fat and any silver skin
Salt to taste
The Mansion on Turtle Creek
Pepper Mixture (see page 261)

3 tablespoons peanut oil
  Ancho Chili Sauce
  Jicama–Black Bean Garnish
¹⁄₄ cup fresh cilantro leaves, washed
  and dried

Season fillets with salt and Pepper Mixture to taste.

Heat oil in a large sauté pan over medium-high heat. Place several fillets in hot pan. Do not crowd (cook in batches if necessary). Brown one side, turn, and brown other side. Cook to desired degree of doneness, about 3 minutes on each side for medium-rare. Remove from heat and keep warm.

Ladle Ancho Chili Sauce over the bottom of each of four warm dinner plates. Place 2 beef medallions on each plate. Sprinkle Jicama Black–Bean Garnish evenly around meat. Sprinkle with cilantro leaves.

ANCHO CHILI SAUCE

4 dried ancho chilies, stemmed and
　seeded (if peppers are small, use 1
　more)
1 tablespoon peanut oil
1 yellow onion, cut into medium
　dice
2 shallots, chopped
2 cloves garlic, chopped
1 jalapeño chili, seeded and
　chopped

3 sprigs fresh cilantro
1 cup chicken stock (see page 262)
1 medium tomato, chopped
1/2 cup brown veal demi-glace (see
　page 263)
1/2 cup heavy cream
1/2 tablespoon honey or to taste
　Salt to taste
　Juice of 1/2 lime or to taste

Place chilies in a bowl and cover with hot water. Soak for 30 minutes, then drain.

Heat oil in a medium saucepan over medium heat. Add onion and sauté 2 minutes. Add shallots, garlic, and jalapeño and sauté for 2 minutes longer. Add cilantro, chicken stock, and tomato; simmer for 12 minutes. Add demi-glace, increase heat slightly, and cook for about 10 minutes or until liquid is reduced by half. Add cream and heat just to boiling.

Pour hot mixture into a blender or food processor and process until smooth. Add honey to taste, increasing amount slightly if sweeter sauce is desired. Season to taste with salt and lime juice. Keep warm.

JICAMA—BLACK BEAN GARNISH

1 tablespoon peanut oil
1 cup medium-diced jicama (see
　page 271)
1 red bell pepper, seeded,
　membranes removed, and cut into
　medium dice (see page 271)

1/2 cup cooked black beans
　Salt to taste

Heat oil in a medium sauté pan over medium-high heat. Sauté jicama, pepper, and black beans. Cook for about 2 minutes or just until heated through. Season to taste with salt.

Advance Preparation:
1. Sauce may be made several hours ahead and kept warm. Reheat gently, if necessary.

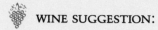 WINE SUGGESTION:

PETIT SYRAH, INGLENOOK, ESTATE BOTTLED, 1982
A lively, full-bodied wine with a black pepper cassis nose and a well-balanced fruity flavor to stand up to this authoritative entrée.

Marinated Grilled Tenderloin of Beef with Tomatillo–Serrano Chili Sauce and Smoked Corn Cakes

Serves 4

This method of marinating was taught to me by our butcher, Gustavo Robles. This traditional Mexican marinade had been handed down through many generations of his family.

8　3½-ounce center-cut beef fillets
　　Juice of 2 limes
3　cloves garlic, minced
1　tablespoon minced fresh cilantro
3　serrano chilies, seeded and minced
1　tablespoon vegetable oil
　　Salt to taste

　　The Mansion on Turtle Creek Pepper Mixture to taste
　　Tomatillo–Serrano Chili Sauce
　　Smoked Corn Cakes
4　clusters of cilantro leaves for garnish

Trim all fat and silver skin from fillets. Place fillets in a single layer in a flat pan for marinating.

In a small bowl, combine lime juice, garlic, cilantro, serrano chilies, and 1 tablespoon oil. Pour over meat and marinate for at least 2 hours, turning fillets occasionally.

Prepare grill. Make sure grates are clean, and lightly rub or brush with oil. Remove meat from marinade, drip dry, and season with salt and Pepper Mixture. Place meat on hot grill and cook for about 3 minutes. Turn each piece and cook for about 3 minutes more for medium-rare. When cooked to desired degree of doneness, remove from grill.

Immediately ladle Tomatillo–Serrano Chili Sauce over the bottom of each of four warm dinner plates. Place 2 beef fillets in the middle of each plate, edges overlapping. Place 2 Smoked Corn Cakes, edges overlapping, beside the meat. Nestle cilantro clusters between the meat and corn cakes. Serve immediately.

TOMATILLO—SERRANO CHILI SAUCE

1 tablespoon olive oil
1 onion, chopped
1 clove garlic, chopped
3 serrano chilies, stems removed
4 sprigs fresh cilantro
1/2 pound tomatillos, husked,
    washed, and chopped

2 cups chicken stock (see page 262)
1 cup heavy cream
4 spinach leaves
    Salt to taste
    Juice of 1/2 lime or to taste

In a medium sauté pan, heat oil over medium heat. Add onion and sauté for about 3 minutes or until wilted. Add garlic and serrano chilies; cook for 1 minute.

Separate leaves from stems of cilantro. Chop stems into fine mince and set leaves aside.

Add tomatillos, cilantro stems, and chicken stock to pan. Bring liquid to a boil, reduce heat, and simmer for 20 minutes, stirring occasionally to prevent tomatillos from sticking. Add cream, bring to a boil, reduce heat, and cook for about 5 minutes or until liquid is reduced by one-third.

Pour mixture into a blender or food processor. Add cilantro leaves and spinach. Process until smooth. Season to taste with salt and lime juice. Strain and keep warm.

SMOKED CORN CAKES

1 ear sweet corn
1 small clove garlic, minced
1 serrano chili, seeded, ribs
    removed, and finely chopped
1 tablespoon finely diced red bell
    pepper (see page 271)
1 tablespoon finely diced yellow
    bell pepper (see page 271)
1 tablespoon finely diced green bell
    pepper (see page 271)
1/2 cup yellow cornmeal

1/2 cup all-purpose flour, sifted
1/2 teaspoon baking powder
1/2 teaspoon salt
1 extra large egg, lightly beaten
1 cup whole milk
1/2 tablespoon bacon grease, melted
    (1 tablespoon salted butter,
    melted, may be substituted)
    Few drops of lemon juice
    About 3 tablespoons vegetable oil

Shuck corn, remove silk, and cut kernels from cob. Place in smoker for 8 minutes (see page 272).

In a medium bowl, combine smoked corn, garlic, serrano chili, and bell peppers. In another bowl, mix cornmeal, flour, baking powder, and salt. Combine egg, milk, and bacon grease. Add vegetables to dry ingredients, then stir in egg mixture. Adjust seasoning with lemon juice. Fold to mix and let rest for 20 minutes. Adjust seasoning, if necessary.

Place a large skillet over medium heat. Add just enough oil to coat bottom of skillet. When skillet is hot, pour corn batter into skillet to make 3-inch corn cakes, about ⅛ cup per corn cake. Cook on 1 side for about 1½ minutes or until brown. Turn and cook until middles of cakes no longer appear wet. Remove cakes to warm platter and repeat to make 8 cakes. Keep warm.

Advance Preparation:
1. Sauce may be prepared several hours ahead and kept warm.
2. Corn cakes may be prepared up to 1 hour before serving and kept warm.

 WINE SUGGESTION:

PINOT NOIR, KNUDSEN-ERATH, VINTAGE SELECT, 1983
Dry, medium-bodied wine with a spicy, cedar nose, and a rich, plummy taste to marry and soften the aggressive flavors of this dish.

Grilled Sirloin Steak with Black Bean "Chili" Sauce

*Serves
4*

*I introduced this "chili" sauce at the "Dallas" cast farewell party
in the summer of 1986 in our world-famous wine cellar. Knowing
how much Larry Hagman loves Texas chili, I wanted to feature a
truly different version.*

4 *8-ounce sirloin steaks*
3 *tablespoons peanut oil*
   Salt to taste

*The Mansion on Turtle Creek Pepper
Mixture to taste (see page 261)
Black Bean "Chili" Sauce*

Trim steaks of all fat and silver skin. Reserve red meat trimmings for sauce.

Have preheated grill ready. Level coals or wood, make sure grates are clean, and lightly rub or brush with oil. Brush steaks with 3 tablespoons peanut oil and season to taste with salt and Pepper Mixture. Grill steaks to desired degree of doneness (3 minutes on each side for medium-rare).

Ladle Black Bean "Chili" Sauce over the bottom of each of four warm dinner plates. Place a steak in the middle of each plate and serve immediately.

BLACK BEAN "CHILI" SAUCE

*4 sprigs fresh cilantro, washed and
dried*
2 tablespoons corn oil
*1 medium onion, peeled and cut
into medium dice (see page 271)*
*1½ green bell peppers, seeded,
membranes removed, and cut into
medium dice (see page 271)*
*½ poblano chili, seeded and cut into
medium dice (see page 271)*
*1 ancho chili, seeded and soaked in
hot water for 20 minutes*
1 serrano chili, seeded and chopped
*1 small jalapeño chili, seeded and
chopped*
1 tablespoon chili powder
2 teaspoons ground cumin
2 teaspoons ground coriander
1 teaspoon paprika
1 clove garlic, chopped

1 cup red wine
*2 tomatoes, cored and diced (see
page 271)*
1 cup chicken stock (see page 262)
*1½ cups brown veal demi-glace (see
page 263)*
Reserved red meat trimmings
Salt to taste
*1 small sweet potato, peeled and
cut into medium dice (see page
271)*
*1 medium red bell pepper, seeded,
membranes removed, and cut into
medium dice (see page 271)*
*1 medium yellow bell pepper,
seeded, membranes removed, and
cut into medium dice (see page
271)*
*1 cup cooked black beans, well
drained*

Separate cilantro leaves from stems. Set aside. In a medium sauté pan, heat 1 tablespoon corn oil and sauté onion, ½ diced green bell pepper, and chilies, over medium heat until they begin to soften. Add chili powder, cumin, coriander, paprika, garlic, and cilantro stems. Sauté for 2 minutes. Add wine and cook until pan is almost dry, stirring frequently to prevent burning.

Add tomatoes, chicken stock, demiglace, red meat trimmings, and salt to taste. Simmer for about 45 minutes or until sauce is reduced by one-third. Strain through a fine sieve and keep warm.

Heat remaining tablespoon corn oil in a sauté pan over medium heat. Sauté potato for about 3 minutes or until soft. Add peppers (including remaining diced green bell pepper) and beans and sauté 2 minutes longer. Stir in cilantro leaves. Scrape mixture into the warm sauce and stir to blend. Use immediately.

Advance Preparation:
1. Black Bean "Chili" Sauce may be prepared several hours ahead and kept warm.
2. Garnish ingredients may be prepared several hours ahead and kept warm. Add vegetables just before serving.

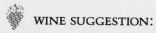 WINE SUGGESTION:

Cabernet Sauvignon, Robert Pepi, Vine Hill Ranch, 1981
An intense, full-bodied wine with a strong cassis nose and predominant taste of currants with hints of tobacco to accompany the peppery rich chili sauce.

Lamb

GRILLED LAMB CHOPS WITH MARJORAM—SMOKED GARLIC SAUCE
AND BARBECUED FIRE-ROASTED ONIONS

ROASTED LOIN OF LAMB WITH SWEET ONION—ROSEMARY SAUCE
SERVED WITH WARM NEW POTATOES AND CARAWAY

GRILLED LAMB CHOPS WITH MARJORAM–SMOKED GARLIC SAUCE AND BARBECUED FIRE-ROASTED ONIONS

*Serves
4*

16 1-inch-thick rib lamb chops,
   butchered in the French style
3 tablespoons peanut oil
  Salt to taste
  The Mansion on Turtle Creek
  Pepper Mixture to taste (see page
  261)

Marjoram–Smoked Garlic Sauce
Barbecued Fire-Roasted Onions
1 small bunch fresh marjoram

Preheat grill. Make sure grates are clean and lightly rub or brush with oil.

Brush chops with 3 tablespoons peanut oil and season to taste with salt and Pepper Mixture. Grill chops about 2 minutes or just long enough to mark one side. Turn chops and cook about 2 minutes longer for medium-rare. Increase cooking time slightly for medium doneness.

Remove chops from grill. If possible, reserve 2 tablespoons of the meat drippings from the pan for use in the Barbecued Fire-Roasted Onions. Spoon Marjoram–Smoked Garlic Sauce over the bottom of each of four warm dinner plates. Place 4 grilled lamb chops along the top of each plate, bones to the center. Place 3 Barbecued Fire-Roasted Onions in a cluster on each plate at the tip of the bones. Garnish plates with sprigs of marjoram beside the onions. Serve immediately with squares of hot corn bread (see page 228).

MARJORAM–SMOKED GARLIC SAUCE

6 large garlic cloves, peeled
1 tablespoon peanut oil
2 large white mushrooms, sliced
  thin
2 shallots, chopped
½ cup brown veal demi-glace (see
  page 263)

1 cup heavy cream
1 small sprig fresh marjoram
3 leaves spinach, rinsed clean
  Salt to taste
  Juice of ½ lemon or to taste

Prepare smoker for smoking vegetables (see page 272).

Immerse garlic cloves in boiling water for 5 minutes. Drain and dry. Place garlic in smoker and smoke for 15 minutes. Set aside.

Heat oil in a medium saucepan over medium-high heat. Add mushrooms and sauté for 1 minute. Add shallots and sauté for 1 minute. Stir in demi-glace and cream. Cook to boiling, then lower heat slightly. Cook for about 10 minutes or until liquid is reduced by one-third or until sauce lightly coats the back of a spoon.

Pour sauce into a blender or food processor and add smoked garlic, marjoram, and spinach. Process until smooth. Strain and season to taste with salt and lemon juice. Keep warm.

BARBECUED FIRE-ROASTED ONIONS

12 medium boiling onions, peeled
1 cup tomato ketchup
4 tablespoons Worcestershire sauce
1 tablespoon malt vinegar
2 tablespoons molasses
2 teaspoons Creole mustard
1 teaspoon Tabasco sauce

1 clove garlic, minced
Salt to taste
Ground black pepper to taste
Juice of ½ lemon or to taste
2 tablespoons meat drippings from grill (if available)

Preheat grill. Make sure grates are clean, and lightly brush or rub with vegetable oil. Place onions on grill. Grill them slowly, turning gradually until lightly charred on all sides, about 30 minutes.

Preheat oven to 375°. Place onions in a small roasting pan. Combine remaining ingredients and pour over onions. Cover and bake in preheated 375° oven for 30 minutes. Carefully turn onions once halfway through cooking time. Remove pan from oven and keep warm.

Advance Preparation:
1. Garlic may be smoked and sauce prepared several hours ahead and kept warm.
2. Onions may be grilled and roasted up to 2 hours before serving and kept warm.

 WINE SUGGESTION:

MERLOT, STERLING, 1983
Dry, full-bodied wine with an oaky cassis nose, firm cherry fruit taste, and rich finish to accompany the distinct smoky flavors of the lamb and sauce.

ROASTED LOIN OF LAMB WITH SWEET ONION–ROSEMARY SAUCE SERVED WITH WARM NEW POTATOES AND CARAWAY

*Serves
4*

*2 1-pound boneless lamb loins, all fat
and silver skin removed
Salt to taste
The Mansion on Turtle Creek Pepper
Mixture to taste (see page 261)*

*1 tablespoon vegetable oil
Sweet Onion–Rosemary Sauce
Warm New Potatoes and Caraway
4 small sprigs fresh rosemary*

Preheat oven to 375°.

Season loins on all sides with salt and Pepper Mixture. Heat oil in a large sauté pan over medium-high heat and brown loins on one side for 2 to 3 minutes. Turn and place sauté pan with lamb in preheated 375° oven. Roast for 8 minutes for medium-rare or to desired degree of doneness. Keep warm. Let loins rest for at least 5 minutes before slicing. Slice about ¼ inch thick, allowing one-half loin per person.

Ladle Sweet Onion–Rosemary Sauce over the bottom of each of four warm dinner plates. Arrange slices of lamb in a semicircle around the middle of the plates, allowing slices from ½ loin per serving. Spoon a small mound of Warm New Potatoes and Caraway in the middle of the semicircle of lamb. Garnish with sprigs of rosemary and serve immediately.

SWEET ONION—ROSEMARY SAUCE

1 tablespoon vegetable oil
1/2 pound lamb bones, chopped into
    small pieces (butcher can do this
    for you)
2 white mushrooms, sliced thin
2 shallots, chopped
1 clove garlic, chopped
3 sprigs fresh thyme
1 cup chicken stock (see page 262)
2 cups brown veal demi-glace (see
    page 263)

1 tablespoon unsalted butter
1 medium sweet East Texas onion
    (or other sweet onion), cut in very
    small dice (see page 271)
2 tablespoons dry sherry
    Salt to taste
    Juice of 1/2 lemon or to taste
1 small sprig fresh rosemary

Heat oil in a large saucepan over medium-high heat. Add bones and sauté for about 10 minutes or until light brown. Add mushrooms and sauté for 2 minutes. Add shallots and garlic and sauté for 1 minute.

Add thyme, chicken stock, and demi-glace. Bring to a boil, reduce heat, and simmer for 30 minutes.

While sauce is simmering, place a medium sauté pan over medium-high heat and add butter. Add onion and sauté until light brown. Add sherry and cook about 10 minutes or until liquid evaporates. Set aside.

After stock has simmered, increase the heat and cook for about 20 minutes or until liquid is reduced by half. Strain through a fine sieve and season with salt and lemon juice to taste. Add onion. Place rosemary in sauce and steep for at least 10 minutes, keeping sauce warm. Remove rosemary before serving.

WARM NEW POTATOES AND CARAWAY

2 tablespoons vegetable oil
1 pound new potatoes, unpeeled,
   sliced ¼ inch thick
   Salt to taste
½ red bell pepper, seeded,
   membranes removed, and cut into
   small dice (see page 271)
½ yellow bell pepper, seeded,
   membranes removed, and cut into
   small dice (see page 271)

½ green bell pepper, seeded,
   membranes removed, and cut into
   small dice (see page 271)
2 teaspoons caraway seeds
2 teaspoons balsamic vinegar

Heat oil in a medium sauté pan over medium-high heat and add potatoes. Season with salt to taste and sauté until potatoes are soft.

Add peppers and caraway seeds and sauté about 3 minutes. Add vinegar and stir to deglaze and loosen all particles from bottom of pan. Remove from heat and adjust seasoning. Keep warm.

 WINE SUGGESTION:

PINOT NOIR, SAINTSBURY, 1983
A delicate but full-flavored wine with good berry nose and soft, fruity, and slightly smoky taste to enhance the subtle presentation and flavor of the lamb.

Game

ROASTED BOB WHITE QUAIL MARINATED IN MOLASSES AND GINGER,
SERVED WITH TANGERINE-LEEK SAUCE

ROASTED QUAIL WITH APPLE, HONEY, AND THYME SAUCE

ROASTED TEXAS PHEASANT WITH LLANO ESTACADO
ZINFANDEL—APPLE SAUCE AND WALNUT—COUNTRY HAM COMPOTE

ROASTED TEXAS PHEASANT WITH SAUCE OF 1984 PHEASANT RIDGE
CABERNET SAUVIGNON AND WHOLE GRAIN MUSTARD

TEXAS "BROKEN ARROW" VENISON WITH SPICY GOLDEN PEAR
SAUCE AND WILD RICE COMPOTE

VENISON MEDALLIONS WITH BLACKBERRY-SAGE SAUCE
AND COMPOTE OF LEEK AND WILD MUSHROOMS

ROASTED BOB WHITE QUAIL MARINATED IN MOLASSES AND GINGER, SERVED WITH TANGERINE-LEEK SAUCE

Serves 4

Quail has always been a special Texas bird. The raising of it was one of the first "cottage" industries to supply The Mansion on Turtle Creek's restaurant. The quail we use are now grown specifically for us in tiny, "just a spot on the road," Blanket, Texas.

8 6-ounce quail
2 tablespoons molasses
1 tablespoon grated fresh ginger
1 clove garlic, minced
2 sticks cinnamon
1 tablespoon white wine vinegar
1 cup fresh tangerine juice
   Salt to taste

The Mansion on Turtle Creek Pepper Mixture to taste (see page 261)
3 tablespoons peanut oil
2 tablespoons unsalted butter
1 cup sliced shiitake mushrooms
   Tangerine-Leek Sauce
8 6-inch chive strips

To ease the carving of the breast of cooked birds, remove the wings and wishbone before cooking. Using a sharp boning knife, cut through the main wing joint and detach wing. Then pull back neck skin to locate the wishbone. Using the tip of the boning knife, carefully follow the outline of the wishbone along the front of the breast about 1/4 inch deep. Use your fingers to gently remove wishbone intact. Use wings and wishbone to make stock.

Combine molasses, ginger, garlic, cinnamon, vinegar, and tangerine juice and mix well. Pour over quail and marinate for 4 hours, covered and refrigerated. Turn quail occasionally to flavor all sides evenly.

Remove birds from marinade and reserve liquid. Place quail on paper towel and allow to drain.

Preheat oven to 375°.

Season quail inside and out with salt and Pepper Mixture to taste. Heat oil in a large ovenproof sauté pan over medium-high heat and brown birds on all sides.

If sauté pan is large enough to hold all

8 birds, place pan with quail in preheated 375° oven. If larger pan is needed, place birds in roasting pan and roast for 8 to 10 minutes or until juices run clear. Do not overcook and dry out the birds.

Remove quail and allow to cool enough to handle. Remove legs and thighs from quail in one piece; reserve and keep warm. Using the sharp tip of a knife, separate breast meat from bone by running knife between meat and bone along the length of the breast bone. Remove breasts in two halves.

Melt butter in a small sauté pan over medium-high heat. Stir in sliced shii-take mushrooms and sauté for 3 minutes or until slightly wilted. Remove from heat and keep warm.

Ladle Tangerine-Leek Sauce over each of four warm dinner plates to cover the bottom of the plate; sprinkle leek strips over sauce. Allow 2 quail per plate (4 legs and 4 breasts). In pairs, crisscross the legs at the 10 o'clock and 2 o'clock positions. From the center of each plate, fan out the breasts to the 4, 5, 7, and 8 o'clock positions on plates. Place equal portions of sautéed mushrooms in the center of each plate. Crisscross two chive strips over all and serve immediately.

TANGERINE-LEEK SAUCE

*1 tablespoon peanut oil
Reserved wings and wishbones from quail
2 shallots, chopped
1/2 cup fresh tangerine juice
Reserved liquid from marinade
1/2 cup brown veal demi-glace (see page 263)*

*4 tablespoons cold unsalted butter, cut into small pieces
Salt to taste
1 large leek, white part only, rinsed well, cut into fine 1 1/2-inch julienne strips*

Heat oil in a large saucepan over medium-high heat and brown wings and wishbones. Add shallots and sauté for 1 minute. Add tangerine juice, liquid from marinade, and demi-glace. Bring to a boil, skim foam, and reduce heat. Simmer for 20 minutes.

Strain liquid into a clean, medium saucepan. Bring liquid to a boil and cook for 8 minutes or until reduced by two-thirds.

Remove pan from heat and whisk in butter piece by piece. Strain sauce, season to taste with salt, and keep warm.

Fill a medium saucepan halfway with water and bring to a boil over high heat. Add leek and cook for 30 seconds, drain, and keep warm.

Advance Preparation:

1. Sauce may be prepared several hours ahead and kept warm.

2. Quail may be roasted up to 1 hour before serving and kept warm.

 WINE SUGGESTION:

CHENIN BLANC, BOEGER, 1984
A crisp, dry-styled wine with a spicy ginger nose and good acid and balance in the taste to complement the marinade and contrast with the buttery sauce.

ROASTED QUAIL WITH APPLE, HONEY, AND THYME SAUCE

*Serves
6*

*6 8-ounce quail, halved, wings and
wishbone removed (see page 149)
Salt to taste
The Mansion on Turtle Creek
Pepper Mixture to taste (see page
261)
3 tablespoons corn oil*

*¹/₃ cup smoked ham, preferably
Virginia ham, cut into ¹/₄-inch
cubes
1 apple, cored and thinly sliced
18 sprigs fresh thyme
Apple, Honey, and Thyme Sauce*

Preheat oven to 400°.

Season quail halves on all sides with salt and Pepper Mixture to taste. Heat oil in an ovenproof skillet large enough to hold quail in a single layer. Over medium-high heat, cook quail for about 1¹/₂ minutes on one side or until nicely browned. Turn quail and place pan in preheated 400° oven. Roast for about 10 minutes. Remove skillet from oven and sprinkle ham around quail. Cook for about 1 minute on top of stove over high heat. Let quail rest for 5 minutes before serving.

Place 2 quail halves in the center of each of six warm dinner plates (or cut off legs and carefully remove breast meat from each side of quail, allowing 2 breast halves and 2 legs for each serving). Garnish each serving with thin slices of apple, 3 sprigs of fresh thyme, and cubes of ham. Spoon Apple, Honey, and Thyme Sauce around quail and serve immediately.

APPLE, HONEY, AND THYME SAUCE

*2 tablespoons honey
4 sprigs fresh thyme
2 Granny Smith apples, unpeeled,
cored and thinly sliced
2 cups quail or poultry demi-glace
(see page 262)*

*Salt to taste
Juice of ¹/₂ lemon or to taste
1 tablespoon unsalted butter*

Preheat a heavy saucepan over medium-high heat. When pan is very hot, add honey. Pan should be hot enough to caramelize honey immediately. Cook, shaking the pan in a flat, circular motion, until honey takes on the color of dark caramel. *Do not burn.*

Add thyme and apple slices and cook, shaking the pan and stirring the apple slices, for about 2 minutes or until the apple slices are well coated.

Add demi-glace and cook for 15 minutes. Strain through a fine sieve, pressing with a wooden spoon to extract as much of the apple as possible. Reheat sauce, add salt and lemon juice to taste, and swirl in butter just before serving.

Advance Preparation:
1. Sauce may be prepared up to the point of adding butter several hours ahead and kept warm. If necessary, reheat gently. Swirl in butter just before serving.
2. Quail may be roasted and kept warm up to 1 hour before serving.

 WINE SUGGESTION:

CHARDONNAY, INNISFREE, 1985
Full-bodied, dry wine with toasty nose and a fruity taste with spice and apple overtones to complement the caramelized honey and apple flavors of the sauce.

Roasted Texas Pheasant with Llano Estacado Zinfandel–Apple Sauce and Walnut–Country Ham Compote

*Serves
6*

Llano Estacado is a blush-colored Texas zinfandel. I think it is very special, but I have to admit you can use any excellent white zinfandel in this recipe.

3   *2¹/₂-pound pheasants, wings and
    wishbone removed (see page 149)
    Salt to taste
    The Mansion on Turtle Creek Pepper
    Mixture to taste (see page 261)*

4   *tablespoons peanut oil
    Llano Estacado Zinfandel–Apple
    Sauce
    Walnut–Country Ham Compote*

Preheat oven to 400°. Generously season each bird inside and out with salt and Pepper Mixture.

Heat oil in a flat roasting pan large enough to hold three birds. Brown birds on all sides. Place pan in preheated 400° oven and roast pheasants for 20 to 25 minutes. Baste the birds with pan juices at least twice during roasting.

Remove pheasants from oven and allow birds to rest for at least 10 minutes before carving. When birds are cool enough to handle, remove leg and thigh quarters from breasts. Separate drumsticks and thighs at joint. Opposite skin side, make a slit along the length of the thigh bones and remove bones. Reserve boneless thighs. Use drumsticks and thigh bones for pheasant stock, if desired.

Slice the boneless thighs and reconstruct in original shape; keep warm. Next, remove the breast meat from the carcasses to make two boneless halves from each breast. Use the sharp point of a knife to cut between the meat and the bone starting at the widest part of the breast, separating each half. (Prior removal of the wishbone and wings makes this easier.)

Peel off the skin and slice each breast half against the grain, starting with the thicker end. Slice very thin and keep in the shape of the breast halves.

Ladle Zinfandel-Apple Sauce onto the bottom of each of six warm dinner plates. Arrange slices of pheasant from each breast half and a thigh to form a circle in the middle of each plate. Spoon a portion of Walnut–Country Ham Compote in the middle of each plate, so that it is surrounded by breast and thigh meat. Serve immediately.

LLANO ESTACADO ZINFANDEL–APPLE SAUCE

1 Red Delicious apple, cored and sliced thin
1 Granny Smith apple, cored and sliced thin
1 shallot, finely chopped
2 sprigs fresh thyme
¼ cup fine-quality white port wine (preferably California)

1 cup pheasant demi-glace (see page 262)
1 cup Llano Estacado zinfandel
4 raspberries
6 tablespoons very cold unsalted butter, cut into small pieces
Salt to taste
Juice of ½ lemon or to taste

In a large saucepan over medium heat, combine sliced apples, shallot, thyme, port, and pheasant demi-glace. Bring to a boil, reduce heat, and simmer for about 20 minutes or until almost all liquid has evaporated. Remove from heat and set aside.

Place zinfandel in a medium saucepan over medium-low heat and cook for about 8 minutes or until liquid is reduced by half.

Combine apple mixture in saucepan with reduced wine; add raspberries. Remove from fire and whisk in butter piece by piece to form an emulsion. Strain through a fine sieve and season to taste with salt and lemon juice. Keep warm. Do not allow mixture to come to a boil or emulsion will dissolve.

WALNUT—COUNTRY HAM COMPOTE

¹/₂ cup medium-dice (see page 271) lean salt-cured ham (from Missouri, Kentucky, or Virginia or any other Smithfield-type ham)

¹/₂ cup walnut halves
3 tablespoons pure maple syrup
1 tablespoon unsalted butter

Sauté ham and walnuts in a medium sauté pan over medium heat for 2 minutes. Pour in maple syrup and stir to deglaze pan. Cook for 2 minutes. Whisk in butter making sure it is incorporated into mixture. Keep warm.

Advance Preparation:
1. Pheasants may be roasted up to 1 hour before serving and kept warm.
2. Sauce may be prepared up to 1 hour before serving and kept warm.

 WINE SUGGESTION:

CHARDONNAY, MERRYVALE, 1984
A dry, medium-bodied wine with a slight oaky nose and clean fruit flavors to complement the apple and nut overtones of the dish.

ROASTED TEXAS PHEASANT
WITH SAUCE OF 1984 PHEASANT RIDGE CABERNET SAUVIGNON AND WHOLE GRAIN MUSTARD

*Serves
4*

2 *2¹/₂-pound pheasants, wings and
wishbone removed (see page 149)
Salt to taste
The Mansion on Turtle Creek Pepper
Mixture to taste (see page 261)*

2 *tablespoons peanut oil
Sauce of 1984 Pheasant Ridge Cabernet Sauvignon and Whole Grain
Mustard*

Generously season pheasant, inside and out, with salt and Pepper Mixture.

Preheat oven to 425°.

Heat oil in a large ovenproof sauté pan over medium heat. Cook pheasant for about 5 minutes per side to brown. Arrange in pan, breast side up, and place in preheated 425° oven for 12 to 15 minutes, or until juices run clear. Baste at least twice during cooking.

Remove from oven and allow birds to rest for at least 10 minutes before carving. Remove legs and thighs, separate and discard drumsticks. Using sharp point of a knife, loosen thigh meat from bone and discard bone, maintaining thigh in 1 piece, including skin. Keep thigh portions warm. Using the sharp point, run a knife between meat and bone to separate breast meat from carcass in two halves.

Thinly slice thigh meat, including skin. Remove skin from breast and slice breast thinly against the grain.

Ladle Sauce of 1984 Pheasant Ridge Cabernet Sauvignon and Whole Grain Mustard over the bottom of each of four warm dinner plates. Arrange slices of pheasant breast in a semicircle around top of plate and place sliced thigh meat in a fan shape behind the breast. Serve immediately.

SAUCE OF 1984 PHEASANT RIDGE CABERNET SAUVIGNON AND WHOLE GRAIN MUSTARD

1 *tablespoon peanut oil*
3 *white mushrooms, sliced*
2 *shallots, chopped*
1 *tablespoon cracked black peppercorns*
3 *sprigs fresh thyme*
2 *cups 1984 Pheasant Ridge Cabernet Sauvignon (or other good-quality cabernet sauvignon)*

1 *cup pheasant demi-glace (see page 262)*
1 *tablespoon whole grain mustard*
   Salt to taste
   Juice of ½ lemon or to taste

Heat oil in a medium saucepan over medium heat. Sauté mushrooms, shallots, and peppercorns about 2 minutes. Add thyme and cabernet; cook until liquid is reduced by two-thirds. Add pheasant demi-glace and bring to a boil. Strain through a fine sieve and stir in mustard. Season to taste with salt and lemon juice.

Advance Preparation:
1. Sauce may be prepared several hours ahead and kept warm. Gently reheat if necessary.
2. Pheasant may be roasted up to 1 hour before serving and kept warm. Slice just before serving.

 WINE SUGGESTION:

CABERNET SAUVIGNON, PHEASANT RIDGE, 1984
A dry, medium-bodied wine with an oak, bell pepper nose and fruity, well-structured finish to accompany the predominantly wine-flavored sauce.

TEXAS "BROKEN ARROW" VENISON WITH SPICY GOLDEN PEAR SAUCE AND WILD RICE COMPOTE

Serves
6

Mike Hughes and Perrin Wells of Broken Arrow Ranch, which supplies most of our game, take me on the most interesting and educational hunting trips down through Mike's "small" 700-acre ranch.

18 2½-ounce medallions from the saddle of venison (backstrap fillets)
Salt to taste
The Mansion on Turtle Creek Pepper Mixture to taste (see page 261)

6 tablespoons peanut oil
Spicy Golden Pear Sauce
Wild Rice Compote

Season fillets with salt and Pepper Mixture to taste. Heat 3 tablespoons oil in a large sauté pan over medium-high heat. Place as many fillets in pan as you can without crowding.

Cook fillets for 1 to 2 minutes on each side, just to seal surface and brown edges. Meat should be medium-rare.

Repeat as needed to sauté all fillets.

Ladle Spicy Golden Pear Sauce over the bottom of each of six warm dinner plates. Place 3 venison fillets at 3 points on the plate to form a triangle, leaving a space in the center of the plate. Spoon a mound of Wild Rice Compote in the center of each plate. Serve immediately.

SPICY GOLDEN PEAR SAUCE

3 mushrooms, sliced thin
1 tablespoon peanut oil
3 shallots, minced
6 golden pears (Bartlett or Anjou),
  cored and sliced thin
4 sprigs fresh thyme
1 tablespoon crushed black
  peppercorns

1 tablespoon crushed green
  peppercorns
2 serrano chilies, seeded
1 cup white port wine
2 cups brown veal demi-glace (see
  page 263)
Salt to taste
Juice of 1 lemon or to taste

Sauté mushrooms in oil in a large saucepan over medium-high heat for 1 minute, or just until they begin to release their juices. Add shallots and sauté another minute.

Add pears, thyme, peppercorns, serrano chilies, and port. Bring liquid to a boil and cook for about 10 minutes or until all liquid has evaporated. Add demi-glace and bring to a boil.

Remove from heat and strain through a fine sieve. Season to taste with salt and lemon juice. Keep warm.

WILD RICE COMPOTE

1 tablespoon unsalted butter
¼ cup medium-dice lean salt-cured
  ham (see page 271)
½ cup chopped leeks
4 halves sun-dried pears, cut into
  medium dice (see page 271)

2 cups cooked wild rice
1 cup heavy cream
  Salt to taste

Heat butter in a medium sauté pan over medium heat. Add ham and cook for about 4 minutes or until brown. Add leeks and pears. Sauté for 3 minutes but do not brown.

Add cooked rice. (Rice should not be overcooked so that the grains split open.) Stir in cream. Bring liquid to a boil, lower heat somewhat, and cook for about 4 minutes or until cream is thick.

Remove from heat, stir mixture, and season to taste with salt. Keep warm.

Advance Preparation:

1. Sauce may be made several hours ahead and kept warm or reheated gently.

2. Wild rice may be prepared up to 1 hour ahead and kept warm.

 WINE SUGGESTION:

ZINFANDEL, A. RAFANELLI, UNFILTERED, 1983
Big, rich wine with raspberry and pepper nose and long-finishing spicy fruit taste to complement the game flavor and peppery fruit sauce.

Venison Medallions with Blackberry-Sage Sauce and Compote of Leek and Wild Mushrooms

*Serves
4*

8 *3-ounce medallions from the saddle
of venison (backstrap fillets)
Salt to taste
The Mansion on Turtle Creek Pepper
Mixture to taste (see page 261)*

3 *tablespoons safflower oil
Blackberry-Sage Sauce
Compote of Leek and Wild Mush-
rooms*

Season venison with salt and Pepper Mixture to taste. Heat oil in a large sauté pan over high heat. Bring oil to smoking point.

Place medallions carefully in pan and sauté for 3 minutes, being careful not to crowd pan. Turn and cook for another 2 minutes for medium-rare. Repeat as needed to brown all fillets.

Spoon Blackberry-Sage Sauce over the bottom of each of four warm dinner plates. Place 2 venison medallions in center of each plate and nestle a small mound of Compote of Leek and Wild Mushrooms above the medallions. Serve immediately.

BLACKBERRY-SAGE SAUCE

2 *cups zinfandel*
1½ *pints blackberries, rinsed and
well drained (blueberries may be
substituted)*
2 *cups brown veal demi-glace (see
page 263)*

2 *tablespoons unsalted butter
Salt to taste
Juice of ½ lemon or to taste*
2 *sprigs fresh sage*

Place zinfandel in a medium saucepan and bring to a boil. Cook until liquid is reduced to about ½ cup.

Add the berries and return liquid to a simmer. Cook, stirring occasionally, for about 10 minutes or until berries are soft.

Add demi-glace and bring liquid to a boil. Lower heat and cook, stirring occasionally, for 10 minutes or to coat the back of a spoon.

Strain sauce and whisk in butter. Season with salt and lemon juice to taste. Place sage in sauce and steep for 10 to 20 minutes or until ready to use. Keep warm. Remove sage sprigs before serving.

COMPOTE OF LEEK AND WILD MUSHROOMS

1 large leek, white part only
1 cup julienne of assorted wild
  mushrooms (such as morels,
  pleurotes, shiitake, or cepes)

½ cup heavy cream
  Salt to taste
  Juice of ½ lemon or to taste

Cut leek into 2-inch sections. Cut sections into fine julienne strips.

Combine julienne of leeks, wild mushrooms, and cream in a medium saucepan. Bring liquid to a boil, lower heat, and cook for about 5 minutes or until cream has thickened.

Remove from heat and season to taste with salt and lemon juice. Keep warm.

Advance Preparation:
1. Compote may be prepared several hours ahead. Keep warm or reheat gently.
2. Sauce may be prepared several hours ahead. Keep warm or reheat gently if necessary.

 WINE SUGGESTION:

ZINFANDEL, KENDALL-JACKSON, MARIAH VINEYARD, 1984
A medium-bodied wine with rich berry nose and full fruit flavors with a touch of pepper to complement the game and blackberry tastes of the dish.

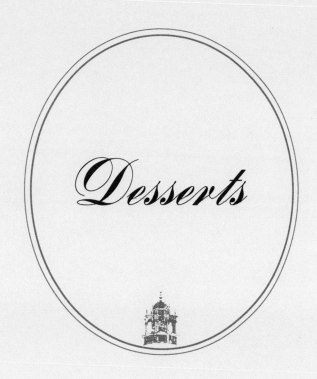

Desserts

Desserts

CRÈME BRÛLÉE

PUMPKIN CRÈME BRÛLÉE WITH FRANGELICO SAUCE

APPLE WALNUT-PECAN TAMALES WITH CRANBERRY-ORANGE GARNISH
AND LATE HARVEST RIESLING WINE SAUCE

BANANA FLIPS

TURTLE CREEK PIE

STRAWBERRY BREAD CUSTARD PIE

PECAN—CHOCOLATE CHIP PIE

MAPLE PECAN AND SWEET POTATO PIE

LATTICE TOP APRICOT—MACADAMIA NUT TART

FRESH FRUIT TART

LIME TARTS

MAPLE PECAN TARTS WITH CARAMEL AND CHOCOLATE SAUCES

BROWN BUTTER BERRY TART

PLUM-BLACKBERRY COBBLER ON SWEET BISCUITS

APPLE AND BLUEBERRY BISCUIT COBBLER

CHOCOLATE SHORTCAKE WITH FRESH FRUIT

CHOCOLATE CARROT CAKE

MOLASSES SPICE CAKE WITH LEMON CURD SAUCE

DOUBLE UPSIDE-DOWN CHOCOLATE CAKE

WHISKEY CAKE

WALNUT—SOUR CREAM CAKE

ITALIAN BLUEBERRY CHEESECAKE

STRAWBERRY CRÈME FRAÎCHE ICE CREAM
WITH LACE COOKIES

CHOCOLATE JACK DANIELS ICE CREAM

NECTARINE ICE CREAM IN A PEANUT TUILE

PUMPKIN ICE CREAM WITH PECAN SAUCE

TEXAS RUBY RED GRAPEFRUIT SORBET WITH
MANGO AND BLACKBERRY SAUCES

CRÈME BRÛLÉE

Serves
6

The mere mention of Crème Brûlée will bring delirious smiles to the face of many of The Mansion on Turtle Creek regulars. The memory of it is indelible. Yet the formula is that of a simple boiled custard poured over raspberries in a puff pastry shell. Sugar is sprinkled over the top before it is run under the broiler. The combination of a crisp caramel shell on top, a tender puff pastry case on the bottom, and a smooth custard interior makes this a rich but soothing dessert.

6 extra large egg yolks
1¼ cups sugar
3 cups heavy cream
1 vanilla bean, split

1 cup raspberries
Puff Pastry
Raspberry Sauce

Combine egg yolks and ½ cup sugar in the top half of a double boiler over very hot water. Whisk (or beat with a hand mixer) until lemon-colored and the consistency of mousse. Remove from heat and set aside.

Place cream and vanilla bean in a heavy saucepan over medium heat. Bring to a boil and immediately remove from heat. Strain through a fine sieve. Slowly pour into egg yolks, whisking rapidly as you pour.

Return double boiler to heat and cook, stirring constantly, for about 10 minutes or until mixture is quite thick. Remove top half of double boiler and place in a bowl of ice. Stir occasionally while mixture cools until it reaches the consistency of a very thick custard.

Spread a single layer of fresh raspberries over the bottom of six baked Puff Pastry shells. Pour cooled crème over raspberries to top of shells. Refrigerate for at least 3 hours (or up to 8 hours). When chilled, sprinkle 2 tablespoons sugar over each filled shell and place about 6 inches away from broiler flame for about 3 minutes or until sugar caramelizes. *Do not overcook or crème will melt!*

Immediately remove from heat. Pour Raspberry Sauce over the bottom of each of six dessert plates. Place a Crème Brûlée in the center and serve immediately.

PUFF PASTRY

*Makes about
1 pound
puff pastry*

2 cups all-purpose flour
  Pinch of salt
1 cup unsalted butter

½ cup ice water, approximately
1 teaspoon lemon juice

Combine flour, salt, and 3 tablespoons butter. Cut butter into flour using a pastry cutter or food processor.

Combine water and lemon juice. Add to flour, mixing to form a pliable dough. Knead by hand for 2 to 3 minutes or process in a food processor until dough forms a ball.

Roll dough on a lightly floured, chilled surface, preferably a marble slab. Surface *must* be chilled. Roll dough to an 8- x 12-inch rectangle. Place pastry with short side facing you. Remaining butter should be cool but malleable. Place butter in center of rectangle and fold the near third of pastry toward the center. Repeat with the far third of pastry to form three layers. Press edges of pastry lightly with a rolling pin to seal. Give pastry a quarter turn and roll again into a rectangle; fold and seal as before. Be careful that butter does not break through during rolling. If

it does, immediately dust lightly with flour and roll again. Wrap and chill at least 15 minutes.

Repeat rolling, folding, and chilling five more times, chilling 30 minutes each time. Chill 1 hour after final rolling.

Preheat oven to 350°.

When pastry is well chilled, roll out as thin as possible on a lightly floured, *chilled* surface. Cut out six 6-inch rounds. Line the ungreased cups of a Texas-size muffin pan (3½ inches x 1½ inches) with the rounds, pressing pastry evenly into cups and trimming edges. Line with a small coffee filter or parchment paper and fill to the top with dried beans (or commercial pastry weights).

Place in preheated 350° oven and bake for 20 to 30 minutes or until pastry is crisp and golden. Remove beans (or weights) and filter (or paper) and allow shells to cool to room temperature.

RASPBERRY SAUCE

1 cup fresh raspberries
¼ cup simple syrup (see page 268)

Purée raspberries in a blender or food processor. When smooth, strain through an extra-fine sieve to remove all seeds. Stir simple syrup into raspberry purée until well blended.

Advance Preparation:
1. Crème may be made up to 3 hours in advance.
2. Puff Pastry shells may be baked up to 3 hours in advance, but do not let them get damp or place them where they can absorb moisture.
3. Raspberry Sauce may be made up to 24 hours in advance.

Pumpkin Crème Brûlée with Frangelico Sauce

*Serves
6*

This is Caroline Hunt's favorite Thanksgiving and holiday dessert. We developed this variation especially for a party she gave at The Mansion on Turtle Creek, and she very graciously made certain that we all knew how much she loved it.

1 cup canned pumpkin
1¼ cups plus 2 tablespoons sugar
⅛ teaspoon salt
½ teaspoon ground cinnamon
¼ teaspoon ground ginger
⅛ teaspoon ground cloves

⅔ cup evaporated milk
6 extra large egg yolks
2½ cups heavy cream
¾ to 1 cup pecan pieces
6 Puff Pastry shells (see page 170)
Frangelico Sauce

Combine pumpkin, ¼ cup sugar, salt, cinnamon, ginger, cloves, and evaporated milk.

Mix egg yolks and ¼ cup plus 2 tablespoons sugar in a double boiler over simmering water, cooking and stirring until lemon-colored and the consistency of mousse. Remove from heat and set aside.

Place cream in a heavy saucepan over high heat and bring to a boil. Immediately remove from heat and pour into egg mixture, whisking briskly. Mixture will appear to separate but will come together as it is whisked.

Return double boiler to heat and cook for about 10 minutes or until mixture is thick and smooth. Stir in pumpkin mixture, blending until it is smooth and creamy.

Remove top half of double boiler and place in a bowl of ice. Stir occasionally while mixture cools until it reaches the consistency of a very thick custard.

Spread a layer of pecan pieces over the bottom of six baked Puff Pastry shells. Pour cooled crème over pecans to top of shells. Refrigerate for at least 3 hours (or up to 8 hours). When chilled, sprinkle 2 tablespoons sugar over each filled shell and place about 6 inches away from broiler flame for about 3 minutes or until sugar caramelizes. *Do not overcook or crème will melt!*

Immediately remove from heat. Pour Frangelico Sauce over the bottom of each of six dessert plates. Place a Crème Brûlée in the center and serve immediately.

FRANGELICO SAUCE

4 extra large egg yolks
¼ cup sugar
2 cups milk
1 vanilla bean, split

¼ cup coarsely ground roasted
*   hazelnuts, skins removed*
⅛ cup Frangelico liqueur, or to taste

Combine egg yolks and sugar in a medium bowl. Place milk and vanilla bean in a heavy saucepan over medium heat and bring to a boil. Immediately remove from heat and cool slightly. Strain through a fine sieve. Slowly pour warm milk into yolks, stirring constantly.

When mixture is well blended, pour into the top half of a double boiler over simmering heat. Cook, stirring constantly, for about 10 minutes or until mixture reaches the consistency of a thick custard.

Remove from heat. Cool, stirring frequently. When cool, stir in hazelnuts and Frangelico liqueur. Serve at room temperature.

NOTE: To remove hazelnut skins before grinding, rub warm, roasted nuts between fingers or rub nuts against each other in a towel.

APPLE WALNUT-PECAN TAMALES
WITH CRANBERRY-ORANGE GARNISH
AND LATE HARVEST RIESLING WINE SAUCE

*Serves
12*

*The use of masa in a dessert recipe is almost unknown in the
United States. In Mexico, however, the dessert tamale is an
everyday sweet. I hope that our Southwest version will encour-
age you to try it.*

24 dried corn husks (see page 257)
   Zest of 1 lemon, finely minced
   Zest of 1 orange, finely minced
1/3 cup simple syrup (see page 268)
1 3/4 cups masa harina (see page 257)
1 teaspoon powdered ginger
4 tablespoons melted unsalted
   butter
2 Granny Smith apples, peeled,
   cored, and coarsely chopped
1/4 cup walnut pieces, coarsely
   chopped

1/4 cup pecan pieces, coarsely
   chopped
2 tablespoons dark raisins
2 tablespoons light raisins
1/2 teaspoon ground cinnamon
1/8 teaspoon ground nutmeg
1/8 teaspoon ground cloves
1/2 cup sugar
2 tablespoons all-purpose flour
   Late Harvest Riesling Wine Sauce
   Cranberry-Orange Garnish

Soak corn husks in hot water to cover for 1 1/2 to 2 hours or until soft and pliable. Make sure husks are separated so that each can absorb plenty of water. Shake off excess water from softened husks before filling.

Combine lemon and orange zests with simple syrup. Heat to boiling, then remove from heat. Place masa harina and powdered ginger in the bowl of a food processor. Using the steel blade, process briefly to combine. Incorporate melted butter until mixture is crumbly. Slowly add simple syrup mixture. Dough should be moist enough to stick together. Add a few drops of water if necessary to make a firm dough. Cover with a towel to prevent drying until ready to make tamales.

Combine apples, walnuts, pecans, and raisins. Mix together cinnamon, nutmeg, cloves, sugar, and flour. Sprinkle dry ingredients over apple-nut mixture. Blend thoroughly and set aside.

Open one corn husk and spread flat. Using wet hands and a small spreader or spatula, spread about 2 heaping tablespoons of masa over the bottom of the husk to cover the center two-thirds, leaving 1/4 inch uncovered on either side. Leave about 3 inches at the pointed end and 1 1/2 inches at the wide end of each husk.

Place 1 tablespoon apple-nut filling in the center of the masa. Fold the sides of the husk together and pinch dough to seal in the filling. Fold bottom and pinch dough to seal. Fold the pointed top down over the filled part to make a tight packet. Repeat with remaining husks. Arrange tamales upright in a large steamer over, but not touching, boiling water. Steam for 20 minutes. When done, remove from steamer and carefully peel away husks.

Ladle Late Harvest Riesling Wine Sauce over the bottom of each of twelve warm dessert plates, reserving enough to drizzle over tamales. Place 2 Apple Walnut-Pecan Tamales on each plate and mound a small spoonful of Cranberry-Orange Garnish on each side. Drizzle a small amount of sauce over each tamale and serve warm.

CRANBERRY-ORANGE GARNISH

1 3/4 cups fresh cranberries
1 cup sugar

2 oranges, zested, peeled, and sectioned

Place cranberries and sugar in a small saucepan over medium heat, with enough water to cover berries halfway. Bring to a boil. Reduce heat and simmer for about 5 minutes or until berries are soft to the touch.

Cover and chill in the refrigerator for about 1 hour. Stir in orange sections just before serving.

LATE HARVEST RIESLING WINE SAUCE

2 cups Late Harvest Riesling
¹/₂ cup unsalted butter, cut into
  pieces, at room temperature

¹/₂ cup heavy cream

Place wine in a small saucepan over medium-high heat and bring to a boil. Reduce heat and simmer for approximately 15 minutes or until liquid is reduced to about 1 cup. Whisk in butter a little at a time until well incorporated. Finally, whisk in cream. If necessary, keep warm over hot, not boiling, water. Serve immediately.

Advance Preparation:
1. Apple Walnut-Pecan Tamales may be prepared up to 2 days ahead and stored in refrigerator. To reheat, wrap tightly in foil and place in 300° oven for 20 to 30 minutes. Tamales may also be frozen. Increase heating time to 40 minutes.
2. Cranberries for the Cranberry-Orange Garnish may be prepared up to 1 day ahead and refrigerated. Stir in orange sections just before serving.

BANANA FLIPS

Serves
8

An upscale version of that old soda fountain favorite, a banana split. It always takes me back to my teenage years at the local Dairy Queen.

2 cups heavy cream
$1/4$ cup sugar or to taste
8 ounces sweet chocolate
8 Éclairs, split in half
    Pastry Cream

3 to 4 bananas, peeled and sliced
    Raspberry Sauce (see page 171)
    Mango Sauce
1 cup fresh raspberries

Whip cream until stiff, gradually adding sugar. Keep cold.

Melt chocolate over hot water (or in a microwave) and dip curved side of "lids" of Éclairs into chocolate or pipe chocolate on tops in a decorative pattern. Set on wax paper to dry.

Fill Éclair bottoms with chilled Pastry Cream, using about $1/4$ cup per serving. Overlap banana slices on Pastry Cream along length of Éclair.

Cover banana slices with whipped cream piped in a spiral design. Gently place chocolate-covered Éclair lid on top.

Pour a small amount of Raspberry Sauce on one half of each of eight dessert plates. Pour a small amount of Mango Sauce on the other half. Place a Banana Flip in the center and garnish with fresh raspberries.

ÉCLAIRS

1 cup milk
¾ teaspoon salt
1 teaspoon sugar

½ cup unsalted butter
1 cup all-purpose flour
1 cup eggs, approximately 5 large

Preheat oven to 400°.

Combine milk, salt, sugar, and butter in a medium saucepan over low heat and slowly bring to a boil. When butter is completely melted, stir in flour and mix vigorously until dough pulls away from the side of the pan and forms a ball. Cook for 1 more minute, stirring constantly.

Transfer dough to the bowl of an electric mixer. Beating at low speed, add eggs, a bit at a time, until all are incorporated. Dough should be shiny and smooth. Place dough in a pastry bag fitted with a ½-inch tube and pipe onto a baking sheet to make eight 5-inch-long, slightly curved "bananas."

Place in preheated 400° oven and bake for approximately 30 minutes or until pastry is crisp to the touch and golden brown in color. Turn off oven. Remove Éclairs from baking sheet and immediately split them horizontally. Scoop out any uncooked dough. Place Éclairs on baking sheet split side down and return to oven (which has been turned off) for about 10 minutes to dry inside.

PASTRY CREAM

2 cups milk
¼ teaspoon pure vanilla extract
⅔ cup sugar

4 tablespoons cornstarch dissolved in 4 tablespoons milk
6 extra large eggs, lightly beaten

Combine milk, vanilla, and ⅓ cup sugar in a small saucepan over medium heat and bring to a boil, stirring frequently. Remove from heat. Combine dissolved cornstarch, remaining ⅓ cup sugar, and eggs. Add a bit of hot liquid to egg mixture, stirring vigorously. Whisk egg mixture into hot milk.

Return pan to heat and cook, stirring constantly, until mixture just comes to a boil. Remove from heat immediately, still stirring. Stir a few minutes off heat. Let cool. Refrigerate for at least 2 hours or until completely chilled.

MANGO SAUCE

¹/₂ cup water
¹/₄ cup sugar

1 to 2 mangoes, peeled and seeded

Combine water and sugar in a small saucepan over medium heat and bring to a boil. Reduce heat and simmer for 5 minutes, stirring occasionally. Remove from heat and let cool. Refrigerate for about 1 hour or until well chilled.

Purée mangoes in a blender or food processor to make 1 cup. Strain through a fine sieve to remove "strings." Stir strained purée into chilled syrup. Refrigerate, tightly covered, until ready to use.

Advance Preparation:
1. Pastry Cream may be made several days ahead, tightly covered, and refrigerated.
2. Fruit sauces may be made up to 1 day ahead, tightly covered, and refrigerated.
3. Éclairs may be made several hours ahead.

TURTLE CREEK PIE

*Makes
1 10-inch pie*

When a guest couldn't make a choice between pecan pie and apple pie, Robert Zielinski, our pastry chef, created this recipe. It is the best of two possible worlds, combining my two favorite desserts.

3 extra large eggs
1 cup sugar
1 cup dark corn syrup
2 tablespoons unsalted butter, melted
1 teaspoon pure vanilla extract

4 Granny Smith apples, peeled, cored, and sliced thin
1 10-inch flan ring, lined with All-Purpose Pastry, unbaked (see page 267)
1/2 cup pecan pieces

Preheat oven to 350°.

Combine eggs and sugar, mixing until sugar is dissolved. Stir in corn syrup, butter, and vanilla. Strain through a fine sieve and set aside.

Place a layer of apple slices in one direction on the bottom of the All-Purpose Pastry shell to form a circle around the outside edge of the shell. Place a second layer inside the first in the opposite direction to form a concentric circle.

Slowly and carefully so as not to disturb slices, pour filling over apples. Sprinkle pecans around outer edge of apples.

Bake in preheated 350° oven for 1 hour. Shield edge with a ring of foil if it begins to get too brown. Return pie to oven and bake for an additional 20 to 25 minutes or until the filling is set. Let cool slightly before cutting.

STRAWBERRY BREAD CUSTARD PIE

*Makes
1 10-inch pie*

4 extra large eggs
½ cup plus 2 tablespoons sugar
3 cups heavy cream
1 cup milk
  Pinch of salt
⅛ teaspoon pure vanilla extract
  Zest of 1 orange

Zest of 1 lemon
5 slices cinnamon raisin bread,
  crusts removed
½ pint strawberries
1 10-inch flan ring, lined with All-
  Purpose Pastry, unbaked (see page
  267)

Combine eggs and ½ cup sugar in a medium bowl and mix until smooth and pale yellow. Stir in 1 cup heavy cream, milk, salt, and vanilla, and blend well. Strain mixture through a fine sieve and add orange and lemon zests. (If time allows, refrigerate overnight for an exceptionally tender custard.)

Preheat oven to 350°.

Cut bread into small cubes and toast in oven for about 10 minutes or until golden brown. Rinse, hull, and halve strawberries, reserving 6 whole berries for garnish.

Place half the halved strawberries and all the toast cubes in the bottom of the unbaked All-Purpose Pastry shell. Top with remaining halved strawberries. Pour custard mixture over berries.

Bake in preheated 350° oven for approximately 45 minutes or until center is set. Cool to room temperature and then refrigerate for about 1 hour.

Combine 2 cups heavy cream and 2 tablespoons sugar. Whip until smooth. Top cold pie with whipped cream and decorate with whole strawberries. Serve immediately.

NOTE: Raspberries, blueberries, or bananas may be substituted for strawberries.

PECAN–CHOCOLATE CHIP PIE

*Makes
1 10-inch pie*

3 extra large eggs, lightly beaten
1 cup sugar
*2 tablespoons unsalted butter,
  melted*
1 cup dark corn syrup
1 teaspoon pure vanilla extract

½ cup chocolate chips
*1 10-inch flan ring, lined with All-
  Purpose Pastry, unbaked (see page
  267)*
1 cup pecans

Preheat oven to 350°.

Combine eggs, sugar, butter, corn syrup, and vanilla in a medium bowl; mix well. Sprinkle chocolate chips over bottom of unbaked All-Purpose Pastry shell. Cover with pecans. Pour filling over chips and pecans.

Bake in preheated 350° oven for 40 to 45 minutes or until a knife inserted halfway between the center and the edge comes out clean. Let set at least 30 minutes before cutting.

MAPLE PECAN AND SWEET POTATO PIE

*Makes
1 10-inch pie*

3 extra large eggs plus 1 egg yolk
½ cup packed light brown sugar
2 tablespoons unsalted butter, melted
1 teaspoon pure vanilla extract
4½ teaspoons pure maple syrup
1½ cups pecan pieces
1 10-inch flan ring, lined with All-Purpose Pastry, unbaked (see page 267)

2½ cups peeled and cubed sweet potatoes
¼ teaspoon ground ginger
¼ teaspoon ground cinnamon
Pinch of ground cloves
2 egg whites
⅓ cup sugar
1 cup unsweetened whipped cream

Preheat oven to 350°.

Combine eggs, egg yolk, and brown sugar in a medium bowl. Stir until sugar is dissolved and mixture is smooth. Blend in butter, vanilla, and maple syrup until well incorporated. Sprinkle pecans evenly over bottom of unbaked All-Purpose Pastry shell. Pour filling into shell. Bake in preheated 350° oven for 30 minutes or until golden brown. Cool to room temperature.

Place sweet potatoes in a large saucepan with enough water to cover and bring to a boil over medium heat. Cook for 15 minutes or until tender; drain. Whip cooked sweet potatoes with ginger, cinnamon, and cloves until almost smooth. You should have about 1½ cups of mashed sweet potatoes. Cool in the refrigerator for 20 minutes.

In a large bowl, beat 2 egg whites until frothy. Gradually add ⅓ cup sugar and continue beating until whites form stiff peaks. Fold meringue into cooled sweet potato mixture.

Gently spoon sweet potato mixture on top of pecan pie and smooth surface. Bake at 350° for 20 minutes or until filling is firm. Remove from heat and cool. Serve cold garnished with unsweetened whipped cream.

LATTICE TOP APRICOT–MACADAMIA NUT TART

*Makes
1 10-inch tart*

1 recipe All-Purpose Pastry (see page
   267)
¼ teaspoon ground ginger
½ teaspoon ground cinnamon
⅛ teaspoon ground allspice
½ cup sugar
¼ cup all-purpose flour
12 fresh apricots, peeled, seeded, and
   diced (do not use canned apricots)

Zest of 1 small lemon
1 tablespoon lemon juice
½ teaspoon almond extract
1½ cups roasted unsalted macadamia
   nuts, finely chopped
1 egg, lightly beaten

Preheat oven to 350°.

Line a 10-inch greased tart pan with All-Purpose Pastry, reserving leftover dough to make a lattice top. Chill lined tart pan in the refrigerator for 15 minutes.

Mix ginger, cinnamon, allspice, sugar, and flour in a large bowl. Stir in diced apricots, lemon zest and juice, almond extract, and nuts, mixing well. Pour into chilled tart shell.

Roll out remaining dough to a ⅛-inch-thick 13-inch round. Cut into ½-inch-wide strips. Beginning in center of pie, place strips from edge to edge, 1 inch apart. Place remaining strips at a 90-degree angle to first strips to form a lattice top. Seal strips to edge. If desired, cut small circles from remaining dough to decorate edge.

Brush lattice top with lightly beaten egg. Bake in preheated 350° oven for 30 to 40 minutes or until golden brown.

FRESH FRUIT TART

*Makes
1 10-inch tart*

1 10-inch flan ring, lined with All-
Purpose Pastry, unbaked (see page
267)
2 cups milk
1/2 cup sugar
1 vanilla bean
3 extra large egg yolks
2 tablespoons all-purpose flour

1 tablespoon cornstarch
1/2 cup heavy cream, whipped
2 cups assorted fresh fruit such as
strawberries, blackberries,
blueberries, peaches, apricots,
Ruby Red grapefruit
1 cup apricot preserves

Preheat oven to 350°.

Place a large coffee filter or parchment paper over All-Purpose Pastry and fill with dried beans (or commercial pastry weights). Bake in preheated 350° oven for 30 minutes. Remove beans (or weights) and filter (or paper) and return to oven for 15 additional minutes or until center is golden. If bottom buckles or bubbles, cover your hand with a heavy towel and use your finger to flatten crust. When golden, remove from oven and set aside.

Combine milk, sugar, and vanilla bean in a small saucepan over medium-low heat. Slowly bring to a boil, then immediately remove from heat.

Combine egg yolks, flour, and cornstarch in a small bowl, mixing well to remove any lumps.

Remove vanilla bean from milk and briskly stir about half the milk into egg

mixture. Quickly combine with remaining milk in saucepan, stirring constantly.

Return saucepan to medium heat and cook, stirring constantly, until thick. Remove from heat. Place a piece of wax paper on surface to prevent skin from forming, and let cool to room temperature. Remove wax paper and refrigerate for at least 2 to 3 hours before using.

When custard is well chilled, fold in whipped cream. Pour into tart shell.

Rinse and thoroughly dry berries. Peel, pit, and slice or divide into sections as required for each variety of fruit. Starting at outside rim of tart shell, arrange fruit on top of custard side by side or in overlapping slices to form concentric circles. In the center of the tart, finish with a fruit that is easy to cut. Alternate fruits of contrasting colors for a dramatic effect.

Melt preserves in a small saucepan over low heat. When thin enough to spread, gently brush or dab preserves over fruit to glaze.

Advance Preparation:

1. Custard may be prepared, without the final whipped cream addition, up to 24 hours in advance.

LIME TARTS

*Makes
8 to 10 3-inch tarts*

*1 recipe All-Purpose Pastry (see page
    267)*
*3 extra large eggs, beaten
    Zest and juice from 3 limes*

³/₄ cup unsalted butter
1³/₄ cups sugar
4 egg whites

Preheat oven to 350°.

Line eight to ten 3-inch tart pans with All-Purpose Pastry. Crimp edges. Place a small coffee filter or parchment paper over pastry and fill with dried beans (or commercial pastry weights). Bake in preheated 350° oven for 15 minutes. Remove beans (or weights) and filter (or paper) and return to oven for 10 additional minutes or until pastry is golden. If bottom buckles or bubbles, cover your hand with a heavy towel and use your finger to flatten crust. When golden, remove from oven and set aside.

Lower oven temperature to 325°.

Beat eggs until thick and lemon-colored. Set aside.

Combine lime zest and juice, butter, and ³/₄ cup sugar in the top half of a double boiler over simmering water. Stir occasionally until butter is melted and sugar is dissolved. Remove from heat.

Vigorously stir a small amount of butter mixture into beaten eggs. Add eggs to butter mixture in top half of double boiler, stirring constantly. Return to heat and cook, stirring constantly, until mixture thickens enough to coat the back of a spoon.

Strain custard through a fine sieve and pour into tart shells. Bake at 325° for 10 minutes. Cool completely; custard will firm as it cools.

Combine egg whites and 1 cup sugar in the top half of a double boiler over simmering water. Stir until sugar is dissolved. Remove from heat and beat until stiff peaks form and whites are thick and glossy in appearance.

Cover tarts with meringue, spreading to seal edges, and place under preheated broiler for about 3 minutes to brown peaks of meringue.

Maple Pecan Tarts with Caramel and Chocolate Sauces

*Makes
8 3-inch tarts*

1 *recipe All-Purpose Pastry (see page 267)*
5 *extra large eggs plus 1 egg yolk*
1 *cup packed light brown sugar*
2 *tablespoons unsalted butter, melted*
2 *teaspoons pure vanilla extract*

3 *tablespoons pure maple syrup*
3 *cups pecan pieces*
  Chocolate Sauce
  Caramel Sauce
1 *cup unsweetened whipped cream*
8 *mint leaves for garnish*

Preheat oven to 350°.

Line 8 3-inch tart pans with All-Purpose Pastry. Crimp edges. Place a small coffee filter or parchment paper over pastry and fill with dried beans (or commercial pastry waights). Bake in preheated 350° oven for 15 minutes. Remove beans (or weights) and filter (or paper) and return to oven for 10 additional minutes or until pastry is golden. If bottom buckles or bubbles, cover your hand with a heavy towel and use your finger to flatten crust. When golden, remove from oven and set aside.

Lightly beat eggs and yolk. Stir in brown sugar and mix until lumps dissolve. Add butter, vanilla extract, and maple syrup. Beat to blend.

Place an equal portion of pecan pieces in each of the eight tart shells, pour filling mixture over nuts, and bake at 350° for 1 hour or until golden brown.

Pour Chocolate Sauce on half of each of eight dessert plates and Caramel Sauce on the other half. Place a tart in the center. Place a dollop of whipped cream on each tart and garnish with a mint leaf on each plate.

CARAMEL SAUCE

*Makes
approximately
2 cups*

¹/₂ cup water
1 cup sugar

1¹/₂ cups heavy cream

Combine water and sugar in a small saucepan over medium heat and bring to a boil, stirring frequently. When liquid begins to boil, lower heat and cook until it turns a golden brown. Immediately remove from heat and slowly stir in cream. (Be careful because hot sauce may splatter.) Serve hot or cold.

CHOCOLATE SAUCE

*Makes
approximately
2 cups*

9 ounces semisweet chocolate
1 cup milk
5 teaspoons heavy cream

¹/₄ cup sugar
2¹/₂ tablespoons unsalted butter

Finely chop semisweet chocolate and place in a heatproof mixing bowl. Set aside.

Combine milk, cream, sugar, and butter in a small saucepan over medium heat. Bring to a boil. Immediately remove from heat and pour over chopped chocolate. Beat until chocolate is melted. Serve hot or cold.

Advance Preparation:
1. Sauces may be made up to 3 days in advance and refrigerated, tightly covered.

Brown Butter Berry Tart

*Makes
1 10-inch tart*

1 recipe Tart Pastry
6 tablespoons unsalted butter
1 vanilla bean
3 extra large eggs

1 cup sugar
⅓ cup all-purpose flour
1 pint fresh raspberries, blueberries,
  or blackberries, washed and dried

Preheat oven to 375°.

Line a 10-inch flan pan with Tart Pastry. Trim edges and crimp lightly.

Combine butter and vanilla bean in a small saucepan over medium heat. Cook for about 10 minutes or until butter turns a golden brown, being careful not to burn. Immediately remove from heat.

Combine eggs and sugar in a large bowl. Add flour and beat until smooth.

Remove vanilla bean from browned butter and pour butter into sugar and flour mixture, blending well.

Spread ½ pint of berries over bottom of dough-lined flan pan. Pour batter over berries. Bake in preheated 375° oven for about 20 minutes or until set.

When done, remove from heat and cool thoroughly. When cool, arrange remaining berries on top. Serve immediately.

TART PASTRY

2 tablespoons plus 2 teaspoons
  sugar
1½ cups all-purpose flour
½ cup very cold unsalted butter

1 egg yolk
2 tablespoons very cold heavy
  cream

Combine sugar and flour in a large bowl. Cut in small pieces of very cold butter, a few at a time, until all butter is used and mixture is crumbly.

Blend egg yolk with cream. Make a well in center of flour mixture, pour in egg mixture, and quickly combine to make a soft dough. Do not overmix or a tough pastry will result.

Roll into a ball, cover with plastic wrap, and refrigerate for 1 hour.

When chilled, roll out to ⅛ inch thickness on a lightly floured surface 2 inches larger than the pan into which pastry will be fitted, or roll and cut to desired size or shape. When fitted into pan, trim edges and finish as directed in individual recipe.

To bake an unfilled tart shell: Preheat oven to 350°. Place a large coffee filter or a large piece of parchment paper over pastry and fill with dried beans (or commercial pastry weights). Bake in preheated 350° oven for 30 minutes. Remove beans (or weights) and filter (or paper) and return to oven for an additional 15 minutes or until golden. If bottom buckles or bubbles, cover your hand with a heavy towel and use your finger to flatten crust.

When golden brown, remove from oven and fill as directed in individual recipe.

Plum-Blackberry Cobbler on Sweet Biscuits

Serves
6

1 pint blackberries, rinsed and well
   drained
4 plums, peeled, pitted, and
   chopped
1/2 cup sugar
1/4 teaspoon ground ginger
1/2 teaspoon ground cinnamon

1/4 teaspoon ground allspice
2 tablespoons all-purpose flour
4 tablespoons unsalted butter
6 Sweet Biscuits
   Vanilla ice cream, if desired
2 tablespoons confectioners' sugar

Preheat oven to 350°.

Combine blackberries and plums in a 1½-quart casserole. Mix sugar, ginger, cinnamon, allspice, and flour. Stir into fruit, mixing gently but thoroughly. Dot with butter. Bake in preheated 350° oven for 25 to 30 minutes or until fruit is soft.

Split Sweet Biscuits in half and place a bottom half on each of six dessert plates. Spoon an equal portion of fruit mixture (warm or room temperature) over each. If desired, place a scoop of ice cream over each serving. Place top of biscuit over cobbler (or lean top against biscuit base and ice cream) and dust biscuit top with confectioners' sugar.

Roasted Bob White Quail Marinated in Molasses and Ginger, Served with Tangerine-Leek Sauce (PAGE 149).

Roasted Texas Pheasant with Llano Estacado Zinfandel–Apple Sauce and Walnut–Country Ham Compote (PAGE 154).

Texas "Broken Arrow" Venison with Spicy Golden Pear Sauce and Wild Rice Compote (PAGE 159).

Desserts displayed in the main dining room. Clockwise from top left: Walnut–Sour Cream Cake (PAGE 202); *Strawberry Bread Custard Pie* (PAGE 181); *Italian Blueberry Cheesecake* (PAGE 203); *Fresh Fruit Tart* (PAGE 185); *Lattice Top Apricot–Macadamia Nut Tart* (PAGE 184).

Crème Brûlée (PAGE 169).

Banana Flip (PAGE 177).

Plum-Blackberry Cobbler on Sweet Biscuit (PAGE 192).

Texas Ruby Red Grapefruit Sorbet, Raspberry Sorbet, and Mango Sorbet with Mango and Blackberry Sauces (PAGE 210).

Afternoon Tea service at The Mansion on Turtle Creek.

Buckwheat Blinis with Caviar (PAGE 239).

SWEET BISCUITS

2 cups all-purpose flour
1/2 teaspoon salt
1 tablespoon baking powder
1/4 cup sugar
2 tablespoons instant nonfat dry milk

1/3 cup chilled vegetable shortening
3/4 cup ice water, approximately
2 extra large eggs

Preheat oven to 350°.

Sift flour, salt, baking powder, sugar, and instant nonfat dry milk into a large bowl. Cut in shortening until mixture resembles cornmeal. Make a well in center of flour mixture and pour in water and 1 egg. Blend until dough holds together.

Turn out onto a lightly floured board and knead several times until dough forms a ball. Roll out to 1/2 inch thickness. Cut with a 4-inch round biscuit cutter to make 6 to 8 biscuits.

Place on an ungreased cookie sheet and brush tops with remaining beaten egg. Bake in preheated 350° oven for 15 to 20 minutes or until sides and bottoms are light brown and top is golden.

Advance Preparation:
1. Fruit mixture may be prepared up to 1 day ahead and stored, tightly covered and refrigerated. May be served at room temperature or gently reheated.
2. Biscuits may be prepared up to 1 day ahead. Store in a covered container.

APPLE AND BLUEBERRY BISCUIT COBBLER

*Serves
8*

You can let your imagination soar when you lay the pattern of the fruit on this cobbler. When you turn it out of the pan you will instantly know whether you are an artist or not.

1 cup packed light brown sugar
1 teaspoon ground cinnamon
2 Granny Smith apples, peeled, cored, and thinly sliced
1 cup blueberries
3 tablespoons lemon juice
³/₄ cup all-purpose flour
¹/₂ cup sugar
1 tablespoon plus 2 teaspoons baking powder

³/₄ teaspoon salt
1¹/₃ cups milk
¹/₃ cup unsalted butter, melted
1 cup cake flour
3 tablespoons vegetable shortening
2 tablespoons very cold unsalted butter

Preheat oven to 350°.

Butter a 10-inch square baking pan. Combine brown sugar and cinnamon. Sprinkle half the mixture evenly over bottom of pan. Arrange apple slices and blueberries in an attractive pattern on bottom of pan and sprinkle lemon juice over fruit. Sprinkle remaining brown sugar mixture over fruit.

Combine all-purpose flour, sugar, 2 teaspoons baking powder, and ¹/₄ teaspoon salt. Add ³/₄ cup milk and beat until smooth. Pour batter over fruit and drizzle with melted butter.

Sift together cake flour, ¹/₂ teaspoon salt, and 1 tablespoon baking powder. Cut in shortening and butter until mixture is crumbly. Stir in remaining milk, a bit at a time, to make a smooth dough.

Roll out biscuit dough on a floured surface to a 10-inch square and place on top of batter. Bake in preheated 350° oven for 35 minutes. Remove from oven and invert onto a serving platter. Let stand for about 3 minutes before removing pan. (You may tap pan bottom a few times to help free cobbler.) When pan is removed, fruit should form an attractive pattern on top. Serve while still warm.

CHOCOLATE SHORTCAKE WITH FRESH FRUIT

Makes
1 9-inch cake

1½ cups sifted cake flour
¾ teaspoon baking soda
¾ teaspoon salt
1⅓ cups sugar
6 tablespoons cocoa powder
½ cup buttermilk

2 extra large eggs, separated
⅓ cup vegetable oil
1 quart heavy cream
2 small bananas
1 pint fresh strawberries

Preheat oven to 350°.

Grease and flour a 9-inch springform pan and line with parchment paper or wax paper. Grease and flour paper. Set aside.

Sift together cake flour, baking soda, salt, ¾ cup sugar, and cocoa. Combine buttermilk and egg yolks. Combine dry and liquid ingredients, alternately adding small amounts of each, to form a batter, beating with an electric mixer at high speed until smooth and free of lumps. Add oil and blend until shiny.

Beat egg whites until they form peaks, gradually adding ¼ cup sugar. Fold beaten egg whites into batter.

Pour batter into prepared pan and bake in preheated 350° oven for 20 to 30 minutes or until a cake tester inserted in center comes out clean.

Let cake cool on rack, then remove from pan. Release sides. Carefully remove bottom and peel off paper. Slice horizontally into 3 layers. Whip cream,

gradually adding ⅓ cup sugar, until stiff. Keep cold.

Peel and slice bananas. Rinse, dry, hull, and cut strawberries into quarters, reserving a few big strawberries for garnish.

Place bottom layer of cake on a serving platter and cover with whipped cream. Place bananas on cream and spread additional cream over bananas to hold them in place. Add a second layer of cake and spread with whipped cream. Layer strawberries over cream. Spread additional cream to hold strawberries in place.

Add the third layer of cake and cover top with remaining whipped cream. Garnish with reserved whole strawberries. Serve immediately.

Advance Preparation:
1. Chocolate shortcake may be made up to 1 day in advance and stored, tightly covered, in a cool place. Do not cut until ready to use.

CHOCOLATE CARROT CAKE

*Makes
1 10-inch cake*

2 cups packed light brown sugar
1½ cups vegetable oil
4 extra large eggs
2 rounded teaspoons baking soda
1 tablespoon plus 1 scant teaspoon
    ground cinnamon
¾ teaspoon ground nutmeg

Pinch of salt
¼ cup plus 1 tablespoon cocoa
    powder
1¾ cups all-purpose flour
1 pound carrots, peeled and grated
½ pound chopped walnuts
4 ounces white chocolate

Preheat oven to 350°.

Grease and flour a 10-inch tube pan.

Combine brown sugar, oil, and eggs, stirring until smooth. Sift together baking soda, cinnamon, nutmeg, salt, cocoa powder, and flour. Beat dry ingredients into liquid, mixing well.

Fold in carrots and walnuts. Pour batter into prepared pan and bake in preheated 350° oven for 45 to 50 minutes or until a cake tester inserted near center of ring comes out clean.

Cool in pan on rack for 15 minutes. Turn out cake and let cool completely.

Melt white chocolate in the top half of a double boiler over hot water or in a microwave and pour over top of cooled cake.

If desired, garnish with melted dark chocolate (drizzled or piped on with a pastry bag) and fresh fruit such as strawberries.

MOLASSES SPICE CAKE WITH LEMON CURD SAUCE

*Makes
1 9-inch cake*

My friend Bradley Ogden, chef at Compton Place in San Francisco, came to Dallas to present a cooking seminar. This dessert, which he brought with him, reminded me so much of my childhood that I asked if I could use it at The Mansion on Turtle Creek.

2¾ cups cake flour
 1 tablespoon ground ginger
 ½ teaspoon ground cinnamon
 ½ teaspoon ground nutmeg
 ½ teaspoon ground cloves
 ¼ teaspoon salt
 1 teaspoon baking soda

½ cup unsalted butter
 1 cup molasses
 ½ cup packed dark brown sugar
 1 cup buttermilk
 ¼ cup freshly squeezed orange juice
 2 extra large eggs, slightly beaten
   Lemon Curd Sauce

Preheat oven to 350°.

Grease and flour a 9-inch round cake pan.

Sift together dry ingredients in a large bowl and set aside. Melt butter in a small saucepan over low heat, then stir in molasses and brown sugar. Set aside to cool.

When butter mixture is cool, stir into dry ingredients and mix until smooth. Add buttermilk, orange juice, and eggs. Beat with an electric mixer at medium speed for about 2 minutes or until smooth and shiny.

Pour batter into prepared cake pan and bake in preheated 350° oven for 35 to 40 minutes or until a cake tester inserted in center comes out clean.

Invert onto cake rack. Remove pan and cool cake slightly. When ready to serve, cut into wedges. Place cake wedges on dessert plates and spoon a generous portion of Lemon Curd Sauce over the top of each.

LEMON CURD SAUCE

Zest and juice of 2 large lemons
1 cup sugar
4 tablespoons unsalted butter

2 extra large egg yolks
2 extra large eggs

Combine zest and juice of lemons, sugar, butter, egg yolks, and eggs in a small saucepan over medium heat. Whisk constantly until thickened. Strain through a fine sieve and cool slightly before serving.

DOUBLE UPSIDE-DOWN CHOCOLATE CAKE

*Makes
1 10-inch cake*

3/4 *cup unsalted butter, softened*
1/2 *cup packed light brown sugar*
1/2 *cup light corn syrup*
1/2 *cup chopped pecans (or walnuts)*
1 *cup sugar*
1 *extra large egg, separated*
2 *ounces unsweetened chocolate,
    melted*

1 1/4 *cups all-purpose flour*
1 *tablespoon baking powder*
1/4 *teaspoon salt*
3/4 *cup milk*
1 *teaspoon pure vanilla extract*

Preheat oven to 350°.

Grease a 10-inch round layer cake pan and line it with parchment or wax paper. Grease and flour paper. Set aside.

Cream 1/2 cup butter and brown sugar, beating until fluffy. Add syrup and nuts and stir until well incorporated. Spread on bottom of prepared pan and set aside.

Cream together 1/4 cup butter and sugar, beating until fluffy. Beat in egg yolk and melted chocolate.

Sift together flour, baking powder, and salt.

Alternately add sifted dry ingredients and milk to creamed mixture, beginning and ending with dry ingredients. Continuing to mix, add vanilla.

Beat egg white until stiff and fold into batter. Pour batter over nut mixture and bake in preheated 350° oven for 40 to 50 minutes or until a cake tester inserted in center comes out clean.

Cool on rack for 15 minutes and turn out onto a serving platter, nut topping side up. Gently peel off paper. Serve warm or at room temperature.

Whiskey Cake

Makes
1 5- × 9-inch loaf

¹/₄ cup water
1¹/₄ cups plus 2 tablespoons sugar
¹/₂ cup plus ²/₃ cup bourbon whiskey
1¹/₂ cups all-purpose flour
1 teaspoon baking powder
¹/₄ teaspoon salt
¹/₂ cup unsalted butter
3 extra large eggs, separated

2 teaspoons ground nutmeg
³/₄ cup coarsely chopped black walnuts
¹/₂ cup black raisins
Chocolate Cream
¹/₂ cup chopped mixed black and English walnuts for garnish, if desired

Preheat oven to 325°.

Grease a 5- × 9-inch loaf pan and line with parchment paper or wax paper. Grease and flour paper. Set aside.

Combine water and ¹/₄ cup sugar in a small saucepan over medium heat. Bring to a boil and boil for 5 minutes. Add ¹/₂ cup bourbon whiskey. Remove from heat and set aside.

Sift together 1 cup flour, baking powder, and salt. Cream butter and 1 cup sugar, mixing until fluffy. Add egg yolks, one at a time, beating well after each addition. Add nutmeg.

Alternately add sifted dry ingredients and ²/₃ cup bourbon to creamed mixture in small amounts, beginning and ending with flour.

Combine walnuts, raisins, and ¹/₂ cup flour. Stir into batter.

Beat egg whites with 2 tablespoons sugar to form soft peaks. Fold whites into batter and pour into prepared pan. Let stand for 5 minutes. Bake in preheated 325° oven for 1 hour or until a cake tester inserted in center comes out clean.

Cool 1 hour on rack before turning out of pan.

After cake is completely cool, cut loaf in half horizontally. Soak bottom layer with half the reserved whiskey syrup. Spread soaked layer with some Chocolate Cream. Reserve enough Chocolate Cream to ice top and sides of cake.

Place remaining layer on top of chocolate cream and soak top layer with rest of whiskey syrup. Frost cake on sides and top with Chocolate Cream. If desired, place any remaining Chocolate Cream in a pastry bag fitted with a star tip and decorate top. Garnish sides with chopped nuts, if desired.

CHOCOLATE CREAM

8 ounces semisweet chocolate
3 tablespoons unsalted butter, melted

2 cups whipped cream

Melt semisweet chocolate in the top half of a double boiler over hot water or in a microwave. Stir in butter. Allow to cool. Fold in whipped cream and immediately ice cake.

Walnut–Sour Cream Cake

*Makes
1 10-inch cake*

2 cups unsalted butter
3 cups packed brown sugar
1/4 cup molasses
4 extra large eggs
2 teaspoons pure vanilla extract
4 cups all-purpose flour
2 teaspoons baking powder
1 1/2 teaspoons ground cardamom

1/2 teaspoon salt
2 1/2 teaspoons baking soda
2 cups sour cream
1 tablespoon ground cinnamon
1 cup chopped walnuts
Lemon Glaze
2 tablespoons confectioners' sugar

Preheat oven to 350°.

Grease and flour a 10-inch tube pan.

Cream butter and 2 1/2 cups brown sugar in a large bowl until fluffy. Continue beating while adding molasses, eggs, and vanilla.

Sift together flour, baking powder, cardamom, salt, and baking soda. Alternately add sour cream and flour mixture to batter, beginning and ending with flour mixture. Do not overmix.

Combine 1/2 cup brown sugar, cinnamon, and 3/4 cup walnuts and set aside.

Spoon enough batter into prepared pan to cover the bottom. Dot with dollops of reserved brown sugar mixture. Add a layer of batter and top with additional dollops of brown sugar mixture. Cover with a final layer of batter.

Bake in preheated 350° oven for 1 hour or until a cake tester inserted near center of ring comes out clean.

Allow cake to cool in pan on a rack for 15 to 20 minutes. While still warm, turn onto a serving platter.

Spread Lemon Glaze over top of warm cake and sprinkle with additional chopped nuts. When cake has cooled, sift confectioners' sugar over top.

LEMON GLAZE

1 1/2 cups confectioners' sugar
1/4 cup lemon juice (fresh orange juice may be substituted)
1 teaspoon pure vanilla extract

Combine confectioners' sugar with lemon juice and vanilla. Beat until smooth. Use immediately.

ITALIAN BLUEBERRY CHEESECAKE

*Makes
1 8-inch cake*

2 cups graham cracker crumbs
1 1/2 cups sugar
1/4 cup melted unsalted butter
1 teaspoon ground cinnamon
8 ounces cream cheese
2 extra large eggs plus 1 egg yolk
8 ounces mascarpone cheese
8 ounces ricotta cheese, sieved

3 tablespoons toasted ground
  unsalted almonds
1 tablespoon lemon zest
1/2 teaspoon pure vanilla extract
1/2 teaspoon almond extract
1/2 cup fresh blueberries (frozen may
  be substituted but do not defrost)

Preheat oven to 325°.

Combine graham cracker crumbs, 1/2 cup sugar, butter, and cinnamon, mixing until well blended. Press into bottom and up sides of an 8-inch springform pan. Bake in preheated 325° oven for 8 minutes. Remove from oven and set aside.

Cream together cream cheese and 1 cup sugar. Add eggs and yolk, one by one, beating well after each addition. Beat in mascarpone. Stir in ricotta, nuts, zest, and extracts.

Pour half of cheese filling into graham cracker crust. Top with 1/4 cup blueberries. Pour in remaining cheese filling and spread rest of blueberries on top.

Bake at 325° for 40 to 50 minutes or until filling is set. Turn off oven and allow cake to cool in oven for about 1 hour.

When completely cool, place cheesecake in refrigerator for at least 5 hours or overnight before cutting.

STRAWBERRY CRÈME FRAÎCHE ICE CREAM WITH LACE COOKIES

*Makes
1 quart*

1 cup heavy cream
¹/₂ cup crème fraîche
¹/₂ cup milk
¹/₂ cup sugar
1 extra large egg, lightly beaten

¹/₈ teaspoon pure vanilla extract
*1 pint strawberries, rinsed, hulled,
and roughly chopped*
Lace Cookies

Combine cream, crème fraîche, milk, sugar, egg, and vanilla; stir until sugar is dissolved. Add chopped strawberries and pour into an ice cream maker. Freeze according to manufacturer's directions. Serve with Lace Cookies.

LACE COOKIES

*Makes
3 dozen
cookies*

¹/₂ cup unsalted butter
¹/₂ cup light corn syrup
²/₃ cup packed light brown sugar
3 teaspoons cocoa powder

1 cup all-purpose flour
*²/₃ cup roasted, finely chopped,
unsalted macadamia nuts*
¹/₄ cup vegetable oil

Preheat oven to 375°.
  Grease a cookie sheet.
  Combine butter, corn syrup, and brown sugar in a small saucepan and bring to a boil. Sift together cocoa and flour. Add to boiling mixture and stir well. Stir in macadamia nuts and immediately remove from heat.

Dip a teaspoon in a small amount of oil and spoon out batter in rounds the size of a quarter, placing them 3 to 4 inches apart on prepared cookie sheet. Batter will spread to 2½ to 3 times its original size. Dip spoon in oil frequently to prevent batter from sticking. Bake in preheated 375° oven for 10 to 12 minutes or until cookies are honey-brown in color.

Cool and remove from pan with a spatula.

NOTE: These cookies are also good at tea time.

CHOCOLATE JACK DANIELS ICE CREAM

Makes approximately 1½ quarts

This dessert is every whiskey lover's dream! Being from Kentucky, I also like to make this with good ole Kentucky bourbon.

6 extra large egg yolks
1 cup sugar
1 cup heavy cream
2 cups cold milk

1 vanilla bean, split lengthwise
6 ounces semisweet chocolate
¼ cup Jack Daniels whiskey

Combine egg yolks and sugar in a small bowl, beating until smooth and lemon-colored. Set aside.

Place cream, milk, and vanilla bean in a small saucepan over medium heat and bring to a boil. Immediately remove from heat and cool slightly. Remove vanilla bean and add a small amount of cream to yolks, stirring briskly. Slowly add yolks to remaining cream, stirring constantly. Strain through cheesecloth or a fine sieve.

Melt chocolate over hot water in the top half of a double boiler or in a microwave. Stir into cream mixture and strain once more. Stir in whiskey and chill.

When well chilled, pour into an ice cream maker. Freeze according to manufacturer's directions.

NECTARINE ICE CREAM IN A PEANUT TUILE

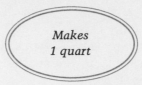

*Makes
1 quart*

5 *extra large egg yolks*
½ *cup plus 1 tablespoon sugar*
1 *cup heavy cream*
¾ *cup milk*
2 *to 3 nectarines, rinsed, peeled,
   and pitted*

1 *teaspoon lemon juice*
Peanut Tuiles
*Mascarpone cheese for garnish, if
desired*
Fresh nectarine sections

Combine egg yolks and ½ cup sugar in a small bowl; beat until smooth and lemon-colored.

Place cream and milk in a small saucepan over medium heat and bring to a boil. Immediately remove from heat. Cool slightly. Add a small amount to yolks, stirring briskly. Stir yolks into remaining cream and milk, stirring constantly. Strain through cheesecloth or an extra fine sieve.

Purée nectarines in a blender with lemon juice and 1 tablespoon sugar. Strain into egg custard. Pour into an ice cream maker and freeze according to manufacturer's instructions. Freeze until hard.

Place scoops of Nectarine Ice Cream in Peanut Tuiles. Garnish with dollops of mascarpone cheese and nectarine sections. Serve immediately.

PEANUT TUILES

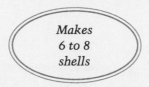

Makes
6 to 8
shells

¼ cup plus 2 tablespoons sugar
1 tablespoon plus 1 teaspoon all-
 purpose flour
2 extra large egg whites

1½ tablespoons melted unsalted
 butter
¼ cup finely ground raw peanuts

Preheat oven to 400°.

Grease a cookie sheet.

Combine sugar, flour, and egg whites in a medium bowl. Beat just until blended. Add butter. Fold in peanuts.

Drop batter by tablespoons onto prepared cookie sheet, allowing several inches between each. Spread batter into 3- to 4-inch rounds using a fork dipped in milk.

Bake in preheated 400° oven for 10 to 15 minutes or until edges are golden brown. Quickly remove tuiles with a spatula and drape over inverted custard cups while still very hot. Cookies will dry crisp to form a cup. You must work quickly. Bake only as many at one time as you can handle while still hot.

Advance Preparation:
1. Peanut Tuiles may be made several hours ahead, but do not let them absorb moisture or they will collapse.

Pumpkin Ice Cream with Pecan Sauce

*Makes
approximately
2 quarts*

10 *extra large egg yolks*
1¼ *cups sugar*
2 *cups heavy cream*
1 *vanilla bean, split lengthwise*
1 *cup pumpkin purée*
1 *teaspoon ground cinnamon*

Pinch ground nutmeg
Pinch ground cloves
3 *cups cold milk*
Pecan Sauce
*Whole pecan halves for garnish, if
desired*

Combine egg yolks and sugar in a small bowl, beating until smooth and lemon-colored. Set aside.

Place cream and vanilla bean in a small saucepan over medium heat and bring to a boil. Immediately remove from heat and cool slightly. Remove vanilla bean and add a small amount of cream to yolks, stirring briskly. Slowly add yolks to remaining cream, stirring constantly. Strain through cheesecloth or a fine sieve.

Combine pumpkin, cinnamon, nutmeg, and cloves. Stir into strained mixture and chill.

When well chilled, combine with cold milk and pour into an ice cream maker. Freeze according to manufacturer's directions.

Place scoops of Pumpkin Ice Cream on cold dessert plates. Spoon Pecan Sauce around ice cream and garnish with pecan halves, if desired.

PECAN SAUCE

1 cup whole or broken pecan halves
1/2 cup unsalted butter
1/4 cup sugar

2 tablespoons water
3/4 cup heavy cream

Place pecans in a food processor or blender and process until very fine. Add butter and process until smooth. Measure 1/2 cup and reserve.

Combine sugar and water in a heavy saucepan over medium heat. Bring to a boil and cook, stirring frequently, until sugar mixture becomes the color of dark caramel. Remove from heat and whisk in 1/2 cup pecan butter, then heavy cream.

Return to heat and bring to a boil. Again remove from heat and stir in remaining pecan butter. Cool and serve at room temperature.

Advance Preparation:

1. Pecan Sauce may be made a few hours ahead and kept at room temperature.

Texas Ruby Red Grapefruit Sorbet with Mango and Blackberry Sauces

*Makes
1 quart*

2 cups sugar
1¹/₃ cups water
2 cups very cold fresh Texas Ruby
  Red grapefruit juice

Mango Sauce (see page 179)
Blackberry Sauce

Combine sugar and water in a small saucepan over medium heat and bring to a boil. Stir until sugar is dissolved. Remove from heat, cool, and refrigerate until well chilled.

Combine cold grapefruit juice with 2 cups chilled sugar syrup. Pour into an ice cream maker and freeze according to manufacturer's instructions.

Pour equal portions of Mango Sauce and Blackberry Sauce over each half of a cold dessert plate. Place three small scoops of sorbet at the center of the plate.

NOTE: Two cups of fresh, finely strained raspberry or mango purée may be substituted for grapefruit juice.

BLACKBERRY SAUCE

1 pint blackberries, washed and
  drained dry

Juice of 1 lemon
Sugar to taste

Purée blackberries in a blender until very smooth. Strain through a fine sieve to remove all traces of seeds.

Stir in lemon juice and sugar to taste. Refrigerate, tightly covered, until ready to use.

Special Occasions

Breakfast and Brunch

THE MANSION ON TURTLE CREEK BREAKFAST TACO

EGGS WITH MISSOURI HAM, CHEDDAR CHEESE GRITS, AND FRIED APPLES

TWO EGGS WITH KENTUCKY PORK SAUSAGE, JICAMA HASH BROWNS,
AND JALAPEÑO CORN MUFFINS

BUCKWHEAT GRIDDLE CAKES WITH ROASTED ALMOND MAPLE SYRUP

TEXAS PECAN AND MOLASSES WAFFLES WITH APPLE BUTTER

CINNAMON BRIOCHE FRENCH TOAST

THE MANSION ON TURTLE CREEK GRANOLA

BAKING SODA BISCUITS

CORN BREAD

BREAKFAST PRESERVES

PEAR HONEY

STRAWBERRY PRESERVES

SEEDLESS RED OR BLACK RASPBERRY JAM

RASPBERRY AND RHUBARB CONSERVE

The Mansion on Turtle Creek Breakfast Taco

Serves
4

2 *tablespoons corn oil*
8 *extra large eggs, beaten well*
1 *avocado, peeled, pitted, and cut*
   into small dice (see page 271)
1 *cup finely grated jalapeño Jack*
   cheese
   Salt to taste

   Ground black pepper to taste
4 *Flour Tortillas (see page 6)*
   Green Tomatillo Salsa
   Red Tomato Salsa
   Sprigs of fresh cilantro for garnish,
   if desired

Heat oil in a large skillet (preferably nonstick) over medium heat. When oil is hot, pour in eggs. Slowly stir eggs, scraping bottom and sides of skillet with a rubber spatula.

When eggs begin to take shape, fold in avocado and cheese and season with salt and pepper to taste. When cheese begins to melt, remove from heat.

Lay 1 warm Flour Tortilla on each of four warm dinner plates. Spoon scrambled eggs into the middle of each tortilla. Roll tortillas around eggs in the shape of a cigar and tuck the ends under. Place in centers of plates. Spoon Green Tomatillo Salsa on one side and Red Tomato Salsa on the other side of each tortilla. Garnish with sprigs of fresh cilantro, if desired.

GREEN TOMATILLO SALSA

8 *tomatillos, husked*
1 *clove garlic*
1 *shallot*
1 *serrano chili, seeded*

1 *tablespoon chopped fresh cilantro*
Juice of 1 lime or to taste
Salt to taste

Place tomatillos in a large skillet over medium heat. Cook, shaking frequently, for 10 minutes or until skin starts to split. In a food processor, using the steel blade, chop cooked tomatillos, garlic, shallot, serrano chili, and cilantro very fine or grind in a food grinder to a very fine consistency. *Do not purée.*

Mix well and season to taste with lime juice and salt. If sauce is too thick, thin with a bit of chicken stock.

RED TOMATO SALSA

1½ *very ripe tomatoes, peeled and seeded*
1 *clove garlic*
1 *shallot*

1 *serrano chili, seeded*
1 *tablespoon chopped fresh cilantro*
Salt to taste
Juice of ½ lime or to taste

In a food processor, using the steel blade, chop tomatoes, garlic, shallot, serrano chili, and cilantro very fine or grind in a food grinder to a fine consistency. *Do not purée.*

Mix well and season to taste with salt and lime juice.

Advance Preparation:
1. Salsas may be prepared up to 1 day ahead and refrigerated, tightly covered. Serve at room temperature.
2. Tortillas may be prepared several hours ahead and reheated. Roll and grill tortillas just before serving for maximum freshness. If desired, very fresh factory-made tortillas may be substituted. Wrap in foil and reheat in 300° oven 10 to 15 minutes before serving.

Eggs with Missouri Ham, Cheddar Cheese Grits, and Fried Apples

*Serves
6*

2 tablespoons unsalted butter
6 4-ounce slices salt-cured country
  ham (preferably from Missouri,
  Kentucky, or Virginia)

12 extra large eggs
   Cheddar Cheese Grits
   Fried Apples

Melt butter in a large sauté pan over medium heat. Add ham and brown on 1 side for 3 minutes; turn and cook 2 more minutes. Remove ham from pan and keep warm.

Cook eggs any style, allowing 2 per person.

Place 2 eggs on each of six warm serving plates. Place a slice of ham and a portion of Cheddar Cheese Grits and Fried Apples on each plate.

CHEDDAR CHEESE GRITS

2 cups chicken stock (see page 262)
2 cups water
1 small garlic clove, minced
1 cup quick-cooking (but not instant)
  hominy grits

1 cup grated cheddar cheese
  Salt to taste

Place chicken stock and water in a medium saucepan over high heat. Bring to a boil. Stir in garlic and grits. Reduce heat and simmer, stirring frequently, for about 10 to 15 minutes or until thickened.

Remove from heat and stir in cheese until completely melted. Season to taste with salt and keep warm.

FRIED APPLES

3 tablespoons unsalted butter

4 Granny Smith apples (or any tart green apple), cored and cut into wedges (about 8 pieces per apple)

2 tablespoons light brown sugar

Melt butter in a large sauté pan over medium heat. Sauté apples for about 5 minutes or until they begin to brown.

Add sugar and cook over low heat for about 10 minutes or until sugar caramelizes, being careful not to burn. Apples should have a shiny, candylike appearance. Serve warm.

Advance Preparation:

1. Grits may be prepared several hours ahead and kept warm.
2. Apples may be prepared up to 1 hour ahead and kept warm.

Two Eggs with Kentucky Pork Sausage, Jicama Hash Browns, and Jalapeño Corn Muffins

Serves
6

1 pound lean ground pork
¹/₂ pound ground pork backbone fat
1¹/₂ teaspoons salt
1¹/₂ teaspoons minced fresh sage
³/₄ teaspoon ground black pepper
¹/₈ to ¹/₄ teaspoon cayenne pepper

1 teaspoon minced fresh thyme
¹/₄ teaspoon ground nutmeg
¹/₄ teaspoon fennel seed
12 extra large eggs
Jicama Hash Browns
Jalapeño Corn Muffins

Combine ground pork and fat (or have butcher grind them together). Add salt, sage, black pepper, cayenne, thyme, nutmeg, and fennel. Knead mixture with hands to ensure even mixing. Form a very small test pattie. Cook, then adjust seasoning in raw mixture to taste.

Shape mixture into a roll about 2¹/₂ to 3 inches in diameter. Wrap in wax paper and refrigerate several hours or until firm enough to cut. Refrigerate overnight if desired.

Cut into ¹/₂-inch-thick patties and brown on both sides in a hot skillet making sure sausage is cooked thoroughly. Keep warm.

Prepare eggs any style. Serve with sausage, Jicama Hash Browns, and Jalapeño Corn Muffins.

JICAMA HASH BROWNS

3 cups shredded jicama
1/2 teaspoon minced garlic
1/2 teaspoon minced shallot
1 tablespoon chives cut 1/4 inch long
   Juice of 1 lime

1 tablespoon all-purpose flour
2 extra large eggs, lightly beaten
   Salt to taste
   Ground black pepper to taste
1/4 cup peanut oil, approximately

Drain shredded jicama well. Mix with garlic, shallot, chives, lime juice, flour, eggs, and salt and pepper to taste until well blended.

Scoop 1/4 cup tightly packed jicama into the palm of your hand and form into 3-inch patties.

Heat peanut oil in a medium skillet over medium heat. Place patties in hot oil and lightly brown on 1 side, then turn and cook slowly until jicama is tender on the inside and patties are crisp outside. Use enough oil to keep patties from burning. Serve hot.

JALAPEÑO CORN MUFFINS

1 1/4 cups cornmeal
1 1/4 cups all-purpose flour
1/4 cup sugar
5 tablespoons baking powder
2 1/2 cups milk
8 tablespoons melted salted butter
   (or bacon fat)

2 extra large eggs, lightly beaten
2 teaspoons minced jalapeño chili
1 teaspoon minced garlic
1/4 cup grated cheddar cheese

Preheat oven to 350°.

Lightly grease a 12-cup muffin tin. Combine cornmeal, flour, sugar, and baking powder. Quickly stir in milk, butter or bacon fat, and eggs just to moisten dry ingredients. Do not over-mix.

Fold in jalapeño chili, garlic, and cheese.

Pour batter into prepared muffin

cups, filling three-fourths full. Bake in preheated 350° oven for 10 to 12 minutes or until golden.

Advance Preparation:
1. Jicama mixture may be prepared several hours ahead and fried at the last minute.
2. Jalapeño Corn Muffins may be made several hours ahead and reheated for serving. They may also be made ahead and frozen.

Buckwheat Griddle Cakes with Roasted Almond Maple Syrup

*Serves
6 to 8*

*1 cup buckwheat flour
1 cup all-purpose flour
1 tablespoon baking powder
1/2 teaspoon salt
2 extra large eggs, well beaten*

*1 1/2 cups milk
6 tablespoons unsalted butter,
 melted
Roasted Almond Maple Syrup*

Sift together flours, baking powder, and salt. Add eggs and milk and mix until ingredients are moistened and batter is smooth, but do not overbeat.

Fold in butter. Batter will be thick.

Drop by heaping tablespoons onto a hot, well-greased griddle and brown on one side. Batter will spread to a 3- to 4-inch circle. When bubbles rise on un-cooked surface, turn and brown the other side. Be sure cakes are well browned before turning. Do not turn more than once.

Stack, allowing 3 to 4 pancakes per serving. If desired, slather with butter and serve with hot Roasted Almond Maple Syrup.

ROASTED ALMOND MAPLE SYRUP

*1/2 cup blanched slivered almonds
 2 cups pure maple syrup*

2 sticks cinnamon

Preheat oven to 350°.

Roast almonds in preheated 350° oven for about 5 minutes or until light brown, stirring frequently. Combine roasted almonds, maple syrup, and cinnamon sticks in a small saucepan over low heat. Bring liquid to a simmer. Remove from heat and serve warm.

Advance Preparation:
1. Roasted Almond Maple Syrup may be prepared several hours in advance and reheated.

TEXAS PECAN AND MOLASSES WAFFLES WITH APPLE BUTTER

*Serves
6*

2 cups sifted all-purpose flour
3 teaspoons baking powder
³/4 teaspoon salt
2 extra large eggs, separated
2 tablespoons molasses

1¹/2 cups milk
³/4 cup melted unsalted butter
³/4 cup finely ground pecans
Apple Butter
Pure maple syrup

Sift flour with baking powder and salt. Beat egg whites until they hold soft peaks and set aside.

Beat yolks with molasses and milk. Pour slowly into the dry ingredients, stirring to prevent lumping. Add butter and beat until batter is smooth, then fold in egg whites and pecans.

Bake in a hot waffle iron according to manufacturer's instructions allowing 2 waffles per serving. Serve hot with Apple Butter and pure maple syrup.

APPLE BUTTER

¹/2 cup plus 1 tablespoon unsalted
butter, softened
1 Granny Smith apple, peeled,
cored, and sliced thin

3 tablespoons honey
1 teaspoon ground cinnamon

Heat 1 tablespoon butter in a small sauté pan until foamy. Add apple slices and sauté until very soft but not brown. Add honey and cinnamon. Cook 5 minutes. Force apple through a strainer. Cool, then refrigerate until well chilled.

In a mixer or food processor, combine chilled apple mixture and ¹/2 cup softened butter; process until very smooth. Refrigerate if too soft.

Advance Preparation:
1. Apple Butter may be made several days in advance and refrigerated, tightly covered.

CINNAMON BRIOCHE FRENCH TOAST

*Serves
8*

2 extra large eggs, lightly beaten
²/₃ *cup milk*
¹/₄ *teaspoon salt*
¹/₄ *cup unsalted butter*

*8 1-inch-thick slices Cinnamon
Brioche Loaf
Pure maple syrup*

Beat eggs with milk and salt to blend. Melt about 2 tablespoons of butter in a large, heavy skillet. Dip 1 slice of bread in egg mixture, coating both sides well. Fry for about 1 minute on each side until light brown. Repeat until all slices are brown, adding more butter as needed. Keep warm. Cut slices in half and serve with pure maple syrup (warmed if desired).

CINNAMON BRIOCHE LOAF

*Makes
2 5- × 8-inch
loaves*

2 packages active dry yeast
¹/₄ *cup plus 3 tablespoons sugar*
¹/₂ *cup warm water*
1 teaspoon salt
*8 extra large eggs, at room
temperature*

5 to 5¹/₂ cups all-purpose flour
1¹/₂ cups unsalted butter, softened
2 tablespoons ground cinnamon

Add yeast and ¹/₄ cup sugar to warm water, stirring with a fork to dissolve. Let sit until mixture is foamy.

Place salt and eggs in large bowl of a mixer that has a dough hook. Beat eggs lightly and gradually add flour to make a soft dough, mixing constantly.

With mixer running, add butter, 2

tablespoons at a time, until completely incorporated. Dough will be soft. Using dough hook, knead for about 5 minutes. Dough will be too sticky to knead by hand.

Place in a large, greased mixing bowl. Cover loosely with plastic wrap and a cloth towel. Set in a warm place, free of drafts, to rise for about 1½ hours or until doubled.

When doubled, punch down dough. Cover tightly with plastic wrap and refrigerate 8 hours or overnight.

Grease two 5- × 8-inch loaf pans.

Divide cold dough into 2 pieces. On a lightly floured board, roll each into an 8- × 8-inch square. Combine 3 tablespoons sugar and cinnamon. Sprinkle equal amounts over each piece of dough and roll up as you would a jelly roll. Place in prepared pans.

Cover with a towel and set in a warm place free from drafts to rise for 1 hour or until brioche mounds about 1 inch above edge of pan. Preheat oven to 400°. When brioche has risen, bake in preheated oven at 400° for 30 minutes or until loaf sounds hollow when tapped.

Immediately turn out onto a rack. Cool before cutting.

The Mansion on Turtle Creek Granola

*Serves
10 to 12*

4 cups rolled oats, uncooked (not
  instant)
1/4 cup sliced unsalted almonds
1/4 cup chopped unsalted pistachios
1/8 cup unsalted pine nuts
1/4 cup unsalted sunflower seeds

1/4 cup unsalted pumpkin seeds
1/4 cup unsweetened coconut flakes
1/4 cup honey
2 tablespoons unsalted butter
2 tablespoons light brown sugar
1/4 teaspoon pure vanilla extract

Preheat oven to 325°.

Combine oats, nuts, seeds, and coconut flakes.

Melt honey, butter, and brown sugar in a small saucepan over low heat. Add vanilla. Stir to blend. Place dry ingredients in a roasting pan and pour melted butter mixture over the top. Mix to blend. Place in preheated 325° oven and bake for 15 minutes or until golden, stirring every 5 minutes to keep from burning.

Remove from oven and set aside to cool. Granola will be soggy but will crisp as it cools.

Use hands to break it apart if necessary.

Serve with sliced fresh fruit or berries and heavy cream or milk.

Baking Soda Biscuits

Makes
8 to 10
biscuits

2 *cups sifted all-purpose flour*
¹/₂ teaspoon baking soda
¹/₂ teaspoon salt

4 tablespoons vegetable shortening
³/₄ cup buttermilk

Preheat oven to 475°.

Sift together flour, baking soda, and salt. Cut shortening into dry ingredients until mixture is the texture of cornmeal. Add buttermilk to make a soft dough.

Turn out dough onto a floured surface and knead lightly 2 to 3 times. Roll ¹/₂ inch thick and cut with a floured 2-inch biscuit cutter.

Place biscuits on an ungreased baking sheet and bake in preheated 475° oven for 7 to 10 minutes, until golden brown.

Corn Bread

*Makes
1 10-inch
round bread*

1 cup yellow cornmeal
1 cup all-purpose flour
¼ cup sugar
4 teaspoons baking powder
½ teaspoon salt

1 cup milk
2 extra large eggs, lightly beaten
¼ cup unsalted butter, melted (or melted bacon grease)

Preheat oven to 425°.

Grease a 10-inch cast-iron skillet and place in oven.

Combine cornmeal, flour, sugar, baking powder, and salt. Add milk, eggs, and butter. Stir with a few rapid strokes until dry ingredients are just moistened.

Pour batter into hot pan. Place in preheated 425° oven and bake for 20 to 25 minutes or until edges are light brown and bread is firm.

BREAKFAST PRESERVES

We really do make everything ourselves! Even our jams, jellies, and preserves are made in my kitchen. We think that they are very special and even make breakfast worth getting up early for!

PEAR HONEY

Makes 1¹/₂ pints

¹/₂ pineapple, peeled and cored
4 to 6 pears, peeled and cored

2¹/₂ to 3 cups sugar

In a food processor, using the steel blade, coarsely grate the pineapple and pears. Combine fruits and their juices with sugar in a large, heavy saucepan over medium heat. Bring to a simmer. Reduce heat and cook for about 30 minutes over low heat, stirring frequently to keep from sticking.

When mixture thickens, you can test for spreading consistency by dropping a teaspoon of Pear Honey on a small chilled plate. Place plate in the refrigerator for 2 minutes. If the honey separates and does not run back together when a spoon is pulled through the center, Pear Honey is done.

Immediately remove from heat and pour into 3 sterilized half-pint jars. Store, tightly covered, refrigerated, for up to 4 months. Use as a spread on breads, biscuits, waffles, and pancakes.

STRAWBERRY PRESERVES

*Makes
approximately
1 pint*

1 pint strawberries
2 cups boiling water
1³/₄ cups sugar

1¹/₂ teaspoons vinegar
1 teaspoon lemon juice

Rinse, dry, and hull strawberries. If berries are very large, cut them in half. Place in a large bowl and cover with boiling water. Let stand 5 minutes.

Drain well and place strawberries in a large, heavy saucepan over medium heat. Add ³/₄ cup sugar and stir to melt. Bring to a boil. Add remaining sugar, vinegar, and lemon juice. Stir and bring to a hard boil. Boil rapidly for 15 minutes being careful that jam does not boil over.

Remove from heat, cover, and let stand 12 hours (or overnight). Stir from time to time, if necessary. Pack in a sterilized container. Store, tightly covered, refrigerated, for up to 4 months.

SEEDLESS RED OR BLACK RASPBERRY JAM

Makes approximately 1 pint

1 pint red or black raspberries

1½ cups sugar, approximately

Rinse and dry berries. Force through a fine sieve or strainer to remove most of the seeds. Measure amount of sugar to equal berries and combine with purée in a medium saucepan over medium heat. Bring to a boil. When mixture boils, reduce heat and simmer 20 minutes or until thick.

When mixture thickens, you can test for spreading consistency by dropping a teaspoon of jam on a small chilled plate. Place plate in the refrigerator for 2 minutes. If the jam separates and does not run back together when a spoon is pulled through the center, it is done.

Immediately remove from heat and pour into 2 sterilized half-pint jars. Store, tightly covered, refrigerated, for up to 4 months. Use as a spread on breads, biscuits, waffles, and pancakes.

Raspberry and Currant Jam Variation: Follow the recipe for seedless raspberry jam, using ¾ cup red raspberries to 1¼ cups dried currants. Soak currants in warm water to cover for 30 minutes. Seed and purée berries as above. Drain currants. Combine berry purée and currants to make about 2 cups. Measure amount of sugar to equal combined berries and currants. Combine fruit and sugar in a medium saucepan over medium heat. Proceed as above.

RASPBERRY AND RHUBARB CONSERVE

*Makes
approximately
2 pints*

1 pint red raspberries
1/4 pound red rhubarb stalks

2 1/4 cups sugar

Rinse and drain raspberries. Rinse rhubarb and slice into 1-inch pieces. Place raspberries and rhubarb in a medium saucepan over medium heat. Add sugar, stirring constantly, to melt. Lower heat to simmer and cook for about 20 to 30 minutes or until liquid is quite thick.

When mixture thickens, you can test for spreading consistency by dropping a teaspoon of conserve on a small chilled plate. Place plate in the refrigerator for 2 minutes. If the conserve separates and does not run back together when a spoon is pulled through the center, it is done.

Immediately remove from heat and pour into 4 sterilized half-pint jars. Store, tightly covered, refrigerated, for up to 4 months. Use as a spread on breads, biscuits, waffles, and pancakes.

Tea Time and Cocktails

FINGER SANDWICHES

TEA SCONES

SANDWICH OF SMOKED CHICKEN WITH DAIKON SPROUTS
AND CILANTRO CREAM CHEESE

CRABMEAT SANDWICH WITH ROASTED RED BELL PEPPER—
PECAN CREAM CHEESE

BUCKWHEAT BLINIS WITH CAVIAR

BELGIAN ENDIVE WITH ANTIPASTO SALAD

CUCUMBER WITH SOUR CREAM AND DILL

THE MANSION ON TURTLE CREEK NACHOS

CAVIAR-STUFFED BABY BAKED POTATOES

CHICKEN AND PINEAPPLE BROCHETTE

ARTICHOKES WITH SOUTHWESTERN VEGETABLES

FINGER SANDWICHES

*Makes 16
finger
sandwiches*

1 4-ounce package Boursin herb
 cheese
8 ounces cream cheese, softened
1 tablespoon heavy cream, if
 necessary
4 slices whole wheat bread
4 slices white bread
4 slices dark rye bread

1 tomato, peeled and thinly sliced
1 seedless English cucumber,
 washed, dried, and thinly sliced
1 pound cooked chicken or turkey
 breast, thinly sliced
Leaves from 1 bunch watercress
$1/2$ daikon radish, peeled and thinly
 sliced

Blend together Boursin and cream cheeses until creamy and light. Blend in heavy cream if necessary to make good spreading consistency. Spread cheese mixture generously on one side of each whole wheat and white bread slice.

Spread cheese mixture on both sides of dark rye slices.

Assemble sandwiches in the following order: Cover one slice of white bread (with cheese coating facing up) with sliced tomato and cucumber. Then cover with one slice of dark rye, chicken (or turkey), watercress leaves, and radish slices and top with one slice whole wheat bread (cheese coating facing down).

Repeat until all ingredients are used, making 4 stacks. Trim crusts to make even squares. Cut stacks into 4 fingers or thin rectangles. Refrigerate, covered tightly, several hours or until ready to serve.

TEA SCONES

Makes approximately 12 scones

2 cups all-purpose flour
2 tablespoons sugar
½ teaspoon baking soda
½ teaspoon cream of tartar

½ teaspoon salt
4 tablespoons unsalted butter
1 egg
Approximately ⅚ cup buttermilk

Preheat oven to 400°.

Sift dry ingredients together. With a knife or pastry blender, cut in butter until mixture is crumbly. Place egg in a 1-cup measure and beat lightly. Add enough buttermilk to make 1 full cup.

Stir egg and milk into flour mixture to make a soft dough.

Roll (or pat) out on a lightly floured surface to ½ inch thick. Cut out scones with a 2-inch biscuit cutter and place on ungreased cookie sheet. Bake in preheated 400° oven until slightly puffed and light brown.

Remove from oven and serve immediately with whipped cream and fresh preserves, if desired.

SANDWICH OF SMOKED CHICKEN WITH DAIKON SPROUTS AND CILANTRO CREAM CHEESE

*Makes 16
finger
sandwiches*

¹/₂ cup cream cheese, softened
2 tablespoons minced fresh cilantro
  leaves
12 thin slices whole wheat bread,
  crusts removed

1 small package daikon sprouts or
  radish sprouts
¹/₄ pound smoked chicken breast,
  thinly sliced

Beat cream cheese to a spreading consistency. Fold in cilantro.

Spread cream cheese mixture on one side of each of 4 bread slices. Cover with daikon sprouts. Lightly coat both sides of each of 4 more slices of bread with cheese. Place on top of each daikon-covered slice. Place smoked chicken on top, then finish with a third piece of bread which has been coated lightly with cheese.

Trim crusts to make even squares. Cut into 4 rectangles or triangles.

Refrigerate, tightly covered, until serving, up to several hours.

CRABMEAT SANDWICH WITH ROASTED RED BELL PEPPER–PECAN CREAM CHEESE

*Makes 16
finger
sandwiches*

1 small whole red bell pepper
1/2 cup jumbo lump crabmeat
1/2 cup cream cheese, softened
1/4 cup finely chopped pecans

1/8 teaspoon salt
1 tablespoon lemon juice
12 thin slices white bread, crusts
removed

Roast red bell pepper under broiler or over open flame until skin is blackened on all sides and pepper is soft (see page 261). Pull off charred skin and remove seeds. In a food processor or blender, using the steel blade, purée pulp. Strain through a fine sieve.

Pick over crabmeat to remove any traces of shell or cartilage. Set aside. Whip cream cheese to a spreading consistency. Add pecans, red bell pepper purée, salt, and lemon juice. Mix thoroughly until cream cheese is fluffy and ingredients are well incorporated.

Spread cream cheese mixture on 8 of the bread slices and flake crabmeat over the cheese.

Spread cream cheese mixture on both sides of remaining 4 slices. Assemble sandwich by placing cheese-coated slice between 2 crab-covered slices. Trim crusts to make even squares.

Cut into 4 rectangles, squares, or triangles.

Refrigerate, tightly covered, until serving, up to several hours.

BUCKWHEAT BLINIS WITH CAVIAR

*Makes
6 to 8
servings*

*Beluga, osetra, or sevruga caviar, 1
to 2 ounces per person*
¹/₄ cup finely chopped onion
*¹/₄ cup finely chopped hard-boiled
egg whites*

*¹/₄ cup finely chopped hard-boiled
egg yolks*
Lemon wedges
¹/₂ cup sour cream
Buckwheat Blinis

Nestle caviar in its tin in a bed of shaved ice. Place on a serving platter and surround with small bowls of onion, egg white, egg yolk, lemon wedges, and sour cream. Serve with Buckwheat Blinis on which you should spoon caviar to be topped with any of the garnishes. Use only a bone, wood, or ivory spoon to serve caviar.

BUCKWHEAT BLINIS

*Makes
approximately
36 blinis*

1 cup milk
1/2 tablespoon granulated yeast
4 extra large eggs, separated
1/2 teaspoon salt
1 teaspoon sugar

3 tablespoons melted unsalted
butter
1 1/2 cups sifted buckwheat flour
Vegetable oil or melted unsalted
butter

Scald milk in a small saucepan over medium heat. Remove from heat and cool to lukewarm. Stir in yeast until dissolved and set aside.

Beat egg yolks until thick. Combine with salt, sugar, butter, and yeast mixture. Stir in flour and mix thoroughly.

Beat egg whites until stiff and gently fold into the batter.

Preheat a griddle over medium heat and lightly brush with oil or butter. When hot, pour 1 tablespoon batter onto griddle. Bake for about 2 minutes or until golden brown. Turn and brown other side. Repeat until all batter is used.

If the blinis begin to stick, lightly oil or butter the griddle again.

BELGIAN ENDIVE WITH ANTIPASTO SALAD

*Serves
6*

¼ *cup diced prosciutto ham, cut
from ⅛-inch-thick slices (see page
271)*
¼ *cup diced Genoa salami, cut from
⅛-inch-thick slices (see page 271)*
¼ *cup sliced green olives*
2 *tablespoons toasted pine nuts*
2 *tablespoons grated Romano
cheese*

¼ *cup chopped artichoke hearts
Salt to taste
Ground black pepper to taste*
¼ *cup olive oil, approximately*
1 *teaspoon balsamic vinegar*
1 *tablespoon white wine vinegar*
3 *Belgian endives*

Combine ham, salami, olives, pine nuts, cheese, and artichoke hearts. Season to taste with salt and pepper. Toss with olive oil and vinegars to moisten ingredients.

Cut off root end of endives and separate leaves, using the 12 largest leaves.

Fill leaves with salad mixture. Cover tightly with plastic wrap and refrigerate until ready to serve (or overnight).

NOTE: This salad is appropriate at tea time or with cocktails; allow 2 filled leaves per person.

Cucumber with Sour Cream and Dill

*Serves
10*

4 *English (seedless) cucumbers*
1 *bunch fresh dill, chopped*
1 *cup sour cream*

Salt to taste
Ground black pepper to taste

Cut ends from cucumbers and slice cucumbers in 1-inch-thick rounds to make about 10 slices per cucumber.

Using a small melon baller, scoop a piece out of the center of each slice, being careful not to cut through the bottom. Place cucumber slices scooped side down on paper towel for about 20 minutes to drain off excess liquid.

Combine dill and sour cream, reserving pieces of dill for garnish. Season to taste with salt and pepper.

Fill cucumbers with sour cream, about 1 teaspoon per piece. Sprinkle chopped dill over sour cream or decorate with small dill sprigs.

Refrigerate until ready to serve, up to several hours, tightly covered.

NOTE: These are appropriate at tea time or with cocktails; allow 4 per person.

THE MANSION ON TURTLE CREEK NACHOS

*Makes
48 nachos*

Crisp Tortilla Chips
Mashed Black Beans
Guacamole
2 cups grated Monterey Jack cheese

Very thin slices fresh jalapeño chili
for garnish, if desired
Red Salsa

Preheat broiler.

Spread Crisp Tortilla Chips lightly with Mashed Black Beans. Add a dollop of Guacamole. Top with a sprinkling of cheese. Place under broiler for 1 minute or until cheese melts. Place thin slice of jalapeño chili on each broiled nacho, if desired. Serve with Red Salsa for dipping.

CRISP TORTILLA CHIPS

1 dozen corn tortillas
Approximately 1 cup vegetable oil

Salt to taste

Cut fresh tortillas into quarters. In a deep-sided pan, bring oil to 375° over high heat. Deep fry tortilla quarters for 2 to 3 minutes or until crisp. Drain on paper towel. Salt lightly, if desired.

MASHED BLACK BEANS

1 cup dried black beans
1 onion, chopped
1 clove garlic, chopped
2 to 3 slices bacon, chopped

1 serrano chili, seeded and chopped
3 cups chicken stock (see page 262)
Salt to taste
Ground black pepper to taste

Combine all ingredients except salt and pepper in large saucepan over high heat. Bring to a boil. Reduce heat and simmer, uncovered, for 1½ hours or until beans are tender.

Add salt and pepper to taste. Remove from heat. Cool slightly and place beans in a food processor or blender. Using the steel blade, blend until beans form a chunky paste. If beans have too much liquid, place in a skillet and cook until liquid has evaporated and beans are of a spreading consistency.

GUACAMOLE

3 large avocados
1 jalapeño chili, blanched in hot
   water and seeded
¼ cup finely diced onion

¼ cup finely diced tomato
1½ tablespoons lime juice or to taste
Salt to taste
Ground black pepper to taste

Peel, seed, and mash avocados with a fork. Do not make a smooth purée. Mince jalapeño chili to get 1 tablespoon or to taste. Combine jalapeño with avo-cado and remaining ingredients. Stir to blend. Cover and set aside for at least 30 minutes to allow flavors to meld.

RED SALSA

2 *jalapeño chilies*
1 *onion*
2 *cloves garlic*
4 *medium ripe tomatoes, peeled*
1 *tablespoon chopped fresh cilantro*
   leaves

Salt to taste
Ground black pepper to taste
Juice of ½ lime or to taste

Preheat oven to 350°.

Place jalapeño chilies, onion, and garlic on a baking pan and roast in preheated 350° oven for about 10 to 15 minutes. Chilies should be slightly soft.

Seed and finely chop jalapeño chilies. Peel and finely chop onion and garlic. Chop tomatoes and run through fine blade of a food grinder along with jalapeño chilies, onion, garlic, and cilantro. Season to taste with salt, pepper, and lime juice. Cover and refrigerate until ready to use. Salsa will keep for 2 to 3 days.

Advance Preparation:
1. Guacamole may be made up to 3 hours ahead. Place an avocado seed in prepared Guacamole to prevent discoloring. Cover tightly and refrigerate.
2. Beans may be made up to 2 days in advance and stored, covered and refrigerated.
3. Red Salsa may be made 2 to 3 days in advance and stored, covered and refrigerated.

CAVIAR-STUFFED BABY BAKED POTATOES

*Serves
4 to 6*

I use Idaho potatoes because of their fluffy texture. If baby Idaho potatoes are not available, substitute the moister red or white new potatoes. Size is important—these hors d'oeuvres must be just mouthfuls.

*12 small (1½ to 2 inches) round
  potatoes, preferably Idaho (may
  substitute red or white new
  potatoes)
½ cup sour cream*

*½ cup shredded cheddar cheese
½ cup chopped, crisply fried bacon
½ cup minced fresh chives
 2 ounces beluga, sevruga, or osetra
  caviar*

Preheat oven to 375°.

Scrub unpeeled potatoes well and dry completely. Prick with a fork and place on baking sheet in preheated 375° oven. Bake for about 30 to 40 minutes or until tender.

When done, remove potatoes from oven and cool slightly. Using a mitt or hot pad, gently squeeze potatoes to break up the pulp inside. Cut off tops and use a fork to fluff pulp gently. Scoop out some of the pulp and top each potato with a small dollop of sour cream. Sprinkle with cheese, bacon, and chives. Garnish with a touch of caviar. Serve at room temperature; allow 2 to 3 potatoes per person.

CHICKEN AND PINEAPPLE BROCHETTE

*Serves
8*

¹/₃ cup fresh orange juice
¹/₃ cup water
¹/₃ cup soy sauce
*2 tablespoons oyster sauce
  (available in Oriental markets)*
2 cloves garlic
1 cinnamon stick
2 bay leaves
1 teaspoon ground allspice
1 tablespoon dry mustard
2 tablespoons honey
*1 tablespoon Chinese five spice
  powder*

2 whole cloves
*1 whole chicken breast, skin
  removed*
1 small pineapple, peeled and cored
*1 red bell pepper, seeded and
  membranes removed*
*1 green bell pepper, seeded and
  membranes removed*
1 yellow onion
*1 teaspoon cornstarch dissolved in 2
  teaspoons water*

In a medium saucepan over medium heat, combine orange juice, water, soy sauce, oyster sauce, garlic, cinnamon stick, bay leaves, allspice, mustard, honey, five spice powder, and cloves. Bring to a boil, then immediately remove from heat and set aside to be used as a marinade.

Cut chicken breast off bone, then into small cubes (about 1¹/₂ inches square). Cube pineapple, bell peppers, and onion into uniform shapes of approximately the same size.

Pour just enough marinade over chicken, pineapple, and vegetable cubes to coat, reserving at least ¹/₂ cup. Marinate for 45 minutes to 1 hour.

Preheat oven to 375°.

Remove cubes from marinade, reserving any marinade that remains. Place cubes on wooden skewers, alternating vegetables, pineapple, and chicken for a pleasing appearance.

Place skewers on a jelly roll pan and bake in preheated 375° oven for 10 minutes or just until chicken feels firm. Keep warm.

Place any leftover marinade in a small saucepan. Bring to a boil, then strain through a fine sieve. Return to saucepan (after wiping out any residue), stir in dissolved cornstarch, and heat until thick and bubbly.

Brush thickened sauce on baked brochettes and serve immediately.

ARTICHOKES WITH SOUTHWESTERN VEGETABLES

Serves
6

*¹/₄ cup diced red bell pepper, seeded
and membranes removed (see
page 271)*
*¹/₄ cup diced green bell pepper,
seeded and membranes removed
(see page 271)*
*¹/₄ cup diced yellow bell pepper,
seeded and membranes removed
(see page 271)*
¹/₄ cup diced jicama (see page 271)
¹/₄ cup diced carrot (see page 271)

*¹/₄ cup diced Missouri (or other
smoked) ham (see page 271)*
1 clove garlic, minced
1 shallot, minced
¹/₄ cup olive oil
1 teaspoon balsamic vinegar
1 tablespoon wine vinegar
Salt to taste
Ground black pepper to taste
12 cooked artichoke bottoms

Make certain that the vegetables and ham are of a uniform small dice. Place them in a medium sauté pan with garlic, shallot, and olive oil. Sauté over medium heat just until vegetables are heated through; they should be quite crisp. Remove from heat and cool slightly. Stir in vinegars and salt and pepper to taste. Spoon equal portions into each of 12 cooked artichoke bottoms. Serve immediately; allow 2 per person.

Advance Preparation:
1. Artichokes may be stuffed and refrigerated, tightly covered, up to 24 hours ahead. To reheat, bake at 375° for 20 minutes.

Dean Fearing's Southwest Kitchen

In the Larder

CHILIES

HERBS

FRUITS AND VEGETABLES

GROCERIES

The following brief descriptions should help familiarize you with the basic ingredients of Southwest cuisine. Most of the vegetables, groceries, and herbs required are now available, year-round, throughout the United States. If you should experience difficulty in obtaining the necessary products, one of the sources listed in the back of this section will be able to fill your order promptly.

CHILIES

Fresh chili peppers should always be handled with discretion. After cutting chilies, wash your hands and utensils thoroughly with soap and warm water. You may prefer to wear gloves when working with them. Do not rub your eyes or nose or lick your fingers.

Most of the heat in a chili lies in the interior ribs although each chili can have its own fire spot. If you are concerned about the heat level, eliminate *seeds and membranes* when preparing chilies for cooking. If you follow my recipes as written, you should have no problem with the heat factor. I use chilies as much for their exciting flavor as for their heat level.

FRESH GREEN CHILIES

Jalapeño
A very small, exceptionally hot, smooth green chili; it is perhaps the most popular and widely available. It is frequently pickled. Green cayenne may be substituted.

Poblano
A large, fairly mild, full-flavored chili frequently used for stuffing. California or Anaheim may be substituted.

Serrano
A tiny, fiery-hot, medium-green chili with an intense burn.

Fresh chilies do not store well. I generally recommend that you purchase only what you can use immediately. Long cold storage or freezing will cause heat loss.

DRIED RED CHILIES

Ancho
Dried poblano chili, milder in flavor than other dried chilies.

Cayenne (aka japones)
A small, hot, dried chili often used as a ground pepper.

Dried chilies should be stored tightly covered in a cool, dark spot.

HERBS

Cilantro (aka Chinese parsley, Mexican parsley, coriander)

The most common herb used in Southwest (and Mexican) cooking with a pungent, fresh taste. Usually purchased by the bunch, it can be stored, refrigerated, in a jar of water, covered with a plastic bag for about 1 week. To keep its fresh flavor, cilantro is usually added to a recipe at the last minute because it quickly looses its zest when combined with other foods. There is no substitute for its flavor, and dried coriander, which has a totally different taste, cannot be used.

Epazote (Epasote) (aka wormseed)

A native Mexican herb frequently found growing wild in the United States, it is not yet widely available in markets. There is no exact substitute for its sharp, zesty flavor.

Marigold mint

A native Mexican herb not yet widely available in the United States. Equal portions of fresh mint and fresh tarragon may be substituted.

FRUITS
AND
VEGETABLES

Avocado (aka alligator pear)

A tropical fruit, once known as "Indian butter," now available throughout the United States. Frequently underripe when purchased, avocados can be ripened in 3 to 5 days placed in a closed brown bag in a dark place. There is no substitute for an avocado.

Bell peppers (aka mangoes throughout the midwestern United States)

Mild, sweet peppers with intense colors. I am particularly known for the use of red, green, and yellow bell pepper dice to give color and flavor to my sauces. They are widely available throughout the United States. There is no flavor difference despite color variation.

Chayote (aka christophine, chocho)

A delicate green, pear-shaped squash with a crunchy texture, eaten raw or cooked. Any other crisp, mild squash may be substituted.

Green onion (aka scallions)

The common mild salad onion usually eaten raw. It is widely available year-round. Both white and green parts are edible. Any other mild onion may be substituted.

Jicama

A crunchy root vegetable with pale brown skin and a texture similar to a water chestnut. Its rather sweet flavor is enhanced when chilled. Jicama should not be fibrous or bland. There is no exact substitute.

Mâche (aka lamb's lettuce, field salad)

A delicate salad green most frequently available, imported, in the early spring. To store properly, wash thoroughly, dry, and completely enclose in a tightly sealed container. Refrigerate. Any mild salad green may be substituted.

Mango

A thick-skinned tropical fruit with a soft, succulent, sweet flesh ranging from yellow to pale red in color. Ripe mango clings to its seed and must be carefully peeled and seeded or you will end up with mush. Unripe mango can be eaten cooked. There is no exact substitute.

Papaya

A pear-shaped (or sometimes round) tropical fruit with a pale, rosy-yellow, flowery flesh. It is now widely available throughout the United States. There is no exact substitute.

Passion fruit

A small tropical fruit with a purple-brown, thick rind and a yellow, juicy pulp consisting of seed-filled, small, teardrop-shaped segments. It has an intense, flowery-citrus flavor. There is no exact substitute.

Tomatillo (aka Mexican green tomato or fresadilla)

The basic component of most Mexican green salsas, tomatillos resemble very firm, light green cherry tomatoes with a parchment husk. Almost always roasted or parboiled before using, tomatillos can be eaten raw for a nice acid flavor. They are most frequently available canned, but canned tomatillos will produce an entirely different flavor than fresh.

Tomatoes

Commonly found year-round in all supermarkets. The newer yellow tomatoes are just being introduced across the United States and are my preference for color in salsas and sauces.

GROCERIES

Corn husks

Dried husks (from corn), which must be soaked in warm water for at least 1 hour before using as a cooking wrap for any hand-made filling. Aluminum foil baskets may be substituted.

Masa harina

Lime-soaked, dried corn (hominy), which has been ground for use as a flour in traditional Mexican doughs. There is no substitute.

Tortillas

Made with either flour or cornmeal, tortillas are the bread of Mexico and the Southwest. They are used as a wrap for all types of fillings or served warm at the table. Flour tortillas are easier to work with and blander than those made with corn. Both types are widely available throughout the United States. There is no substitute.

Basic Recipes

THE MANSION ON TURTLE CREEK PEPPER MIXTURE

ROASTED PEPPERS

CHICKEN STOCK (OR PHEASANT OR QUAIL) AND DEMI-GLACE

BROWN VEAL STOCK AND DEMI-GLACE

FISH STOCK

BRINE FOR SMOKING GAME, MEAT, OR FISH

ALL-PURPOSE PASTRY

SIMPLE SYRUP

THE MANSION ON TURTLE CREEK PEPPER MIXTURE

1 cup ground black pepper
$^1/_3$ cup ground white pepper
$1^1/_2$ tablespoons ground cayenne
  pepper

Combine all ingredients. Cover tightly and store in a cool place. Use to season red meats and game before cooking.

ROASTED PEPPERS

Bell pepper (or any other pepper as called for in type and quantity)

Using a fork with a heatproof handle or with the handle wrapped with a towel or hot pad to protect your hand, hold pepper over open flame, such as the burner of a gas stove.

Hold as close as possible without allowing the flames to touch the pepper until the skin puffs and is charred black. Turn as necessary to char the entire pepper.

Immediately place the charred pepper in a plastic bag and seal. Allow pepper to steam for about 10 minutes.

After pepper has steamed, remove from bag and pull off charred skin. Remove stem and seeds. Chop or purée as required in the specific recipe.

If using an electric stove, place whole pepper in a large, dry, cast-iron skillet over medium-high heat. Slowly cook pepper, turning frequently, until charred on all sides. Continue as above.

To roast several peppers at a time, place on a sheet pan under preheated broiler, as close to heat as possible without touching the flames. Roast until skin puffs and is charred black, turning as necessary to char entire pepper. Proceed as above to remove skin and prepare peppers.

Chicken Stock (or Pheasant or Quail) and Demi-Glace

Makes about 4 cups stock or 2 cups demi-glace

1 chicken carcass (or 2 pheasant or
  8 quail carcasses)
2 tablespoons corn, peanut, or
  vegetable oil
1 cup coarsely chopped onion
³/₄ cup coarsely chopped carrots
³/₄ cup coarsely chopped celery
3 sprigs fresh thyme

3 sprigs fresh parsley
1 small bay leaf
1 tablespoon white peppercorns
5 cups water to cover
  For demi-glace: 1¹/₂ tablespoons
  cornstarch mixed with 1¹/₂
  tablespoons cold water

Have butcher cut carcass into small pieces or use a cleaver to do so at home. Heat 1 tablespoon oil in a large saucepan over medium heat. Add carcass. Cook, stirring often, until well browned.

Add remaining oil with onion, carrots, and celery. Cook, stirring frequently, until vegetables are golden brown. Pour off oil. Add thyme, parsley, bay leaf, and peppercorns. Stir to blend and add water to cover.

Bring to a boil, reduce heat, and simmer about 1¹/₂ to 2 hours, skimming surface as necessary, until reduced to 4 cups.

Line a bowl with an extra fine sieve (preferably a chinois). Pour mixture into the sieve and strain, pushing solids with a wooden spoon to extract as much liquid as possible. Discard solids. Skim off any surface fat. Refrigerate, tightly sealed, for no more than 2 days, or freeze in small quantities for ease of use for up to 3 months.

To make demi-glace: Bring finished stock to a boil over high heat. Stir in cornstarch and water mixture, whisking constantly. Lower heat and simmer until reduced to 2 cups or thick enough to coat the back of a spoon. Stir occasionally as demi-glace cools to keep it from separating.

Demi-glace will keep up to 1 week in the refrigerator or for 2 to 3 months in the freezer, tightly sealed. For ease of use, store demi-glace in small quantities.

BROWN VEAL STOCK AND DEMI-GLACE

*Makes 3 quarts
stock or 1 quart
demi-glace*

3 to 4 pounds veal marrow bones,
   cut into 2-inch pieces (or beef or
   venison or lamb)
¾ cup vegetable or olive oil
3 onions, *quartered*
1 carrot, *coarsely chopped*
1 stalk celery, *coarsely chopped*
1 tomato, *quartered*

1 bay leaf
1 tablespoon black peppercorns
2 sprigs fresh thyme
3 crushed garlic cloves
1 gallon water
   For demi-glace: 4 tablespoons
   cornstarch mixed with 4
   tablespoons cold water

Preheat oven to 450°.

Using ¼ cup oil, lightly oil bones. Spread bones in a single layer in a large roasting pan. Place pan in preheated 450° oven and roast, turning occasionally, for about 20 minutes or until bones are dark golden brown on all sides.

When nicely browned, transfer to a large stock pot. Add remaining oil and stir in onions, carrot, celery, and tomato. Cook, stirring frequently, until brown. Add bay leaf, peppercorns, thyme, and garlic.

Pour off fat from the roasting pan. Deglaze pan with 2 cups of water, scraping up any particles sticking to the bottom of the pan. Add this liquid to the stock pot and pour in remaining water. It should cover the bones by 2 inches. Bring to a boil, reduce heat, and let the mixture simmer, uncovered, at least 6 to 8 hours, skimming the foam and fat as necessary. Chill 12 hours or overnight.

Strain the liquid through a sieve into a clean stock pot. Remove any traces of foam or fat. Bring the stock to a rolling boil. Lower heat and cook until the flavor is full-bodied and liquid is slightly reduced. There should be about 3 quarts.

Refrigerate, tightly sealed, for 2 to 3 days or freeze in small quantities for ease of use for 2 to 3 months.

To make demi-glace: Bring finished stock to a boil over high heat. Stir in cornstarch and water mixture, whisking constantly. Lower heat and simmer until reduced to 1 quart or until liquid is thick enough to coat the back of a spoon. Stir occasionally as demi-glace cools to keep it from separating.

Demi-glace will keep up to 1 week in the refrigerator and for 2 to 3 months in the freezer, tightly sealed. For ease of use, store demi-glace in small quantities.

NOTE: If veal bones are used, stock has a neutral flavor and can be used in almost any recipe calling for a mild homemade stock.

FISH STOCK

*Makes
3 quarts*

*1 pound fish skeletons (saltwater
fish such as sole, John Dory,
turbot, halibut, or other very fresh
nonoily fish), cut into pieces*
*2 tablespoons vegetable or other
flavorless oil*
¹/₂ onion, sliced

1 small stalk celery, sliced
1 cup dry white wine
4 cups water, approximately
*1 bouquet garni (2 sprigs each of
fresh parsley and thyme plus 1
small bay leaf tied together)*

Clean the fish bones under cold running water, removing the gills from the head and any traces of blood on the frames.

Heat oil in a large saucepan over medium heat. Add fish bones and vegetables and lower heat. Place a layer of wax paper directly on bones and vegetables in pan and cook over low heat for 10 minutes, stirring once or twice to prevent them from browning.

Remove paper. Add wine, then enough water to cover the bones and vegetables by 2 inches. Add bouquet garni. Raise heat to high and bring to a boil. Skim the surface, reduce heat, and simmer for 20 to 25 minutes.

Strain the stock through an extra fine sieve (preferably a chinois). Refrigerate, tightly sealed, for 2 to 3 days or freeze in small quantities for ease of use, for 2 to 3 weeks. (After 3 weeks the flavor begins to fade.)

BRINE FOR SMOKING GAME, MEAT, OR FISH

1 gallon water
1 cup salt
1 large onion, chopped
1 stalk celery, chopped
1 small carrot, chopped
¹/₄ cup white wine
¹/₄ cup white wine vinegar
2 cloves garlic, chopped

2 serrano chilies, chopped
1 sprig fresh thyme
1 sprig fresh basil
1 sprig fresh tarragon
1 sprig fresh parsley
1 bay leaf
1 2¹/₂-pound pheasant (or other meat or fish)

Combine all ingredients except pheasant in a large stock pot over high heat and bring to a boil. Reduce heat and simmer for 20 minutes. Remove from heat and cool completely. Strain through a fine sieve, reserving brine.

Submerge pheasant in brine and soak for 2¹/₂ hours. (The soaking time required for all game, meat, and fish is 1 hour per pound.) Remove pheasant from brine and shake off excess moisture. Brine may be refrigerated or frozen and used 2 to 3 times for soaking meat or fish for smoking. You may want to boil brine before reusing.

Place pheasant (or other meat or fish) in prepared smoker and smoke according to manufacturer's directions. Smoking time is generally ¹/₂ hour per pound of game, meat, or fish.

ALL-PURPOSE PASTRY

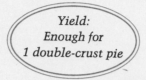

Yield:
Enough for
1 double-crust pie

3 cups all-purpose flour
1 teaspoon salt
3 tablespoons sugar
1 cup very cold unsalted butter, cut
* into pieces*

2 extra large egg yolks, lightly
* beaten*
¹/₄ cup ice water

Combine flour, salt, and sugar. Cut in butter with a knife or pastry blender until mixture resembles coarse meal. Gradually add egg yolks and ice water until a firm ball is formed. Do not overwork dough.

Seal the dough in plastic wrap and chill for at least 30 minutes before rolling out.

When chilled, roll out to about ¹/₈ inch thickness on a lightly floured surface either 2 inches larger than pan into which it will be fitted or cut into desired size or shape. When fitted into pan, trim edges and finish as directed.

SIMPLE SYRUP

Makes approximately 1½ cups

1 cup granulated sugar

1 cup water

Combine sugar and water in a small, heavy saucepan over high heat. Bring to a boil and boil, stirring constantly, for about 3 minutes or until sugar is dissolved. Remove from heat and cool.

May be stored, refrigerated, tightly covered, for up to 3 months.

Techniques

DICING

SMOKING

GRILLING

Throughout the book, I have used specific techniques that enable the home cook to achieve both the look and flavor of the menus at The Mansion on Turtle Creek. None are difficult, but each requires learning a method well and using it whenever a recipe calls for "dicing," "smoking," or "grilling."

DICING

Many of my recipes require cutting vegetables, particularly green, red, and yellow bell peppers, into "small, uniform dice." My signature in garnishes, salsas, and sauces—precisely cut squares of multicolored vegetables adding color and texture—requires a specific cutting technique.

To achieve it, trim ends of vegetables so that pieces are uniform rectangles. These are then cut into very thin strips. For bell peppers, strips should be no more than 1/8 inch wide. The thin strips are then cut into uniform small dice by crosscutting into squares no more than 1/8 inch across. With bell peppers, the ingredient most often requiring this technique, it is important that the inside membrane and seeds be removed and trimmed so the inner walls are very smooth. Absolutely no trace of rib or membrane should remain. For other vegetables a larger dice may be called for, but the same basic technique is applied. It is important that the strips and squares be of uniform size before dicing.

A very sharp paring knife is perfect for trimming, and a small chef's knife (or a boning knife) is the best tool for dicing.

SMOKING

The flavor of smoked foods is integral to Southwest cuisine; many indigenous foods are enhanced by the subtle effects of cooking or flavoring with smoke. This ancient method of cooking and preserving food has been elevated to an art form in the Southwest!

Meats and fish have long been cooked by the smoking process, exposure to low heat and smoke over a long period of time (several hours, even days) to "cook" the meat. But Southwest cuisine has added a new dimension to smoking. Vegetables are very lightly smoked to give them a flavor that is often too subtle for even the most experienced palate to identify but will add an unforgettable accent to food.

Preparation, time, and temperature of the "smoke-cooking" process differ from those of the "smoke-flavoring" process. The former requires soaking the meat or fish in a brine to achieve a full flavor when smoking for a period of time over very low but measurable heat. The latter involves a matter of minutes over "cold smoke."

SMOKE COOKING

The easiest, most reliable smokers to use at home are outdoor cookers sold as "smokers" or "water smokers." The pan that holds the coals is in the bottom of the 2- to 3-foot-tall cooker, about 1½ feet in diameter. A pan—to hold water (or wine for additional flavor) and lower the inside temperature—rests between the coals and the cooking rack. A dome lid traps the smoke.

The smokers, some with two racks for cooking, can easily accommodate whole turkeys, several chickens, ducks, fish, or pheasants, large briskets, or roasts. The food is more flavorful and tender if it has a natural layer of fat to baste the meat as it slowly cooks. Leaving the skin on fish or fowl serves this purpose as does larding lean meats. Most smokers come with explicit instructions for their use, but the rule of thumb to follow when smoking is to allow 1/2 hour smoking time per pound of meat, fish, or game to be smoked.

Wood (such as hickory) or wood charcoal is the preferred fuel. It is more natural and more flavor-intensive than other fuels. Mesquite wood charcoal is my choice at The Mansion on Turtle Creek because it gives the food a true southwestern character.

Charcoal briquettes, especially those infused with liquid starter, can give off fumes that mar the flavors of fresh, delicate foods, and I do not recommend their use. I prefer using a large amount of charcoal so that the coals will burn slowly. I recommend using an electric starter because it imparts no fumes to the charcoal. A chimney starter, fueled by newspaper, is also an acceptable method for firing coals.

Wood chips or pieces (such as hickory, pecan, apple, or cherry) are soaked in water and placed on top of the wood (or wood charcoal) once it has burned down to a gray ash. If the wood is green, it does not need to be soaked before being placed on the gray coals. Dry pieces must be soaked well, however, so they give off smoke instead of burning. This gives the food a wonderful smoky flavor. Any aromatic wood can be used to smoke foods; even fresh herbs, especially woody ones such as rosemary, can be fired. If wood chips burn down, add fresh chips to keep smoke constant.

SMOKE FLAVORING

This process does not cook the vegetables; it flavors them! The vegetables should still be crisp when taken from the smoke. This process can also be used to impart a smoke flavor to meat or seafood, such as sweetbreads or shrimp, which will be cooked through using a different process, often stir-frying.

Several types of outdoor grilling equipment can be used. Before the kitchen at The Mansion on Turtle Creek was equipped with a commercial smoker, I relied on a Weber Kettle Grill. These small, dome-covered cookers are designed primarily for grilling steaks and chickens on decks or patios, but their convenient size and design makes them ideal for imparting a smoke flavor to vegetables usually smoked in small quantities.

Light 4 to 5 pieces of charcoal (a chimney-type starter that uses newspaper to ignite the coals is very handy for this). Mound the hot coals in the bottom of the cooker and let them burn down to gray ash. Spread them into a single layer and lay soaked or green wood chips or pieces (such as hickory, pecan, apple, or cherry) over the ash. You may also use pieces of fresh or dried fruit and/or fresh soaked, dried herbs. This process lowers the heat of the coals to "cold smoke." *Usually, the bottom damper should be closed. The top vent, in the lid, should be open just a crack to draw the smoke.* Place the vegetables to be smoked on the grate above the coals, to the side, not directly over the coals. (When smoking vegetables that have been diced, place them on a layer of foil so they do not fall through.) The grate should be very clean so it does not leave black marks on the vegetables. Smoke for the amount of time specified in each recipe, usually about 20 minutes. If wood chips burn down, add fresh chips to keep smoke constant.

Gas grills can also be used for this process. Preheat one side of the grill for about 10 minutes or until thermostat registers "low." Turn off heat. Place soaked or green wood chips or pieces on the preheated grill rocks. Place the vegetables to be smoked on the cool side of the grill or on the small warming rack that sits above the cooking grate on some models. (When smoking vegetables that have been diced, place them on a layer of foil so they do not fall through.) The grate should be very clean so it does not leave black marks on the vegetables. Smoke for the amount of time specified in each recipe, usually about 20 minutes.

GRILLING

Grilling is a quick-cooking process that seals the food quickly on the outside and cooks it on the inside almost as quickly, although the degree of doneness varies with the food being cooked and individual preferences.

Undercooking is not the problem most often encountered with grilling. In fact, just the opposite usually happens. Many cooks seem to suffer from a widespread and unfounded phobia about food coming off a grill underdone. If the coals are hot enough, this is virtually impossible, particularly with delicate foods such as fish fillets or boneless chicken breast.

Overcooking grilled items is ruinous. It dries out the natural juices, destroying the texture and flavor of the food. And the success of grilling depends on the natural qualities—texture and flavor—coming through to marry with the sauces that I have created to enhance the grilled foods.

At The Mansion on Turtle Creek, high heat is the standard temperature for grilling. Heat is adjusted somewhat, not by allowing the temperature of the fire to rise or fall, but by moving the food on the grill, nearer to or farther from the high heat source.

The heat should be hot enough to "mark" the food immediately when it hits the grill. It should also be hot enough so that cooking a few minutes on one side will seal that surface and cook the food halfway through. The food is then turned and "marked" on the other side, with cooking completed in another few minutes.

Do not be afraid of cooking over hot coals. The coals are ready when flames have died and the coals burn red. If they burn down more, you have waited too long. Throw fresh coals on and wait another 15 or 20 minutes for them to ignite and raise the cooking temperature. I recommend cooking with the bottom vent at least partially open because it helps keep the fire hot. If flames are a problem, however, narrowing the vent opening is one way to control temperature.

On a gas grill, preheat the grill to high for about 10 minutes. It is particularly helpful if your grill has a thermostat to give you a reading on the internal temperature. You can, of course, easily adjust the cooking temperature on a gas grill. But this should not be necessary—and you won't have time—if the grill is hot enough. Move foods to the edges, away from hottest sources of heat, to make minor adjustments. Small pieces that get done first can be placed on the holding rack, which sits toward the back of the grill above the cooking grate on some models, while larger pieces complete cooking.

No matter what equipment is used, the cooking should take only a matter of minutes. Do not make the mistake of placing the lid on the grill and leaving the food to cook. Since the grilling time is short, stand by. Move food away from flare-ups and be prepared to work quickly. If flare-ups persist, lower the lid just long enough to smother the flames. Spraying with water can cause ash to rise and land on the food. *And remember, do not overcook.*

Wood and wood charcoal are becoming widely available and are the fuels of choice. Avoid charcoal briquettes, especially those presoaked with starter fluid, because they can give off fumes that adversely affect the delicate flavor of grilled foods. My choice at The Mansion on Turtle Creek is mesquite wood charcoal for the delicate, characteristic southwestern flavor it imparts.

Cooking over real wood is a bit trickier than using wood charcoal. It tends to flame more and burn with less consistent temperature. It is particularly difficult to work with in a small grill or kettle container.

Just about any home grill equipment can be used if the recommendations for temperature and fuel are followed. Grills fired by wood charcoal give food the subtle flavor of the wood being burned. To achieve this effect with a gas grill, place a chunk or two of mesquite (or other aromatic wood) on the rock bed above the heat source.

Firm-fleshed fish, such as salmon or swordfish, is easiest to grill. When using softer, flakier fish (such as halibut or snapper), be sure the grates are very clean and brushed or rubbed with oil just before the fish is placed on the grill. This lessens the chance that the fish will stick to the grill and tear apart when it is removed. Fish cooks very quickly and is done when the color changes from translucent to opaque. A good rule of thumb when cooking fish is to allow 8 to 10 minutes cooking time per inch of thickness at the thickest part. Since most of the fish fillets prepared in this book are about ½ inch thick, 4 to 5 minutes cooking time is sufficient.

Poultry and game birds take to the grill very well. Again, overcooking is the biggest risk when grilling. Game birds in particular have suffered from cooks' fear of serving underdone meat. They are, in fact, more tender and flavorful if cooked just to the stage where the juices run clear, a medium-rare to medium degree of doneness. Chicken should always be cooked to the point where the juices run clear, but it too suffers when it is cooked too long. Partially or completely boned chicken will sit evenly on the grill and cook quickly and at the same rate throughout.

For optimal flavor and texture, meat, whether beef, lamb, or venison, should never be grilled past the medium-rare stage. Learning to tell by appearance and feel when meat is the proper doneness is a matter of experience. It is much better than cutting into the meat to "look for pink," thereby releasing many of the juices.

Raw meat is soft to the touch and springs back slowly. When meat is the right degree of doneness, it feels firm to the touch and, when gently prodded with a finger, springs back quickly. It looks firm but never coarse or dry. Meat that is overcooked looks rubbery and leathery and does not give to the touch.

Sources

Fresh Herbs
Herb Valley
Ben and JoAn Martinez
204 John McCain Road
Colleyville, Texas 76034
817-498-6362
MasterCard/Visa

Game
Texas Wild Game Cooperative
P.O. Box 530
Ingram, Texas 78025
512-367-5875
MasterCard/Visa
Minimum order $40 plus shipping and
handling

*The Texas Wild Game Cooperative harvests
and markets game meat from more than 80
Texas ranches. Broken Arrow Ranch Venison is one of the game products available
through the cooperative's mail-order service.*

Produce
American Food Service
Lucian LaBarba
4721 Simonton
Dallas, Texas 75234
214-233-5750
MasterCard/Visa

Cheese
Mozzarella Company
Paula Lambert
2944 Elm Street
Dallas, Texas 75226
214-741-4072
MasterCard/Visa

Gourmet Grocery Store
Catalog Available
Simon David
Gift Department
7117 Inwood Road
Dallas, Texas 75209
214-352-1781
MasterCard/Visa

Gift Baskets
Spices, Herbs, Produce
Catalog Available
Goodies from Goodman
12102 Inwood Road
Dallas, Texas 75244
214-387-4804
MasterCard/Visa

Dried Chilies
Crushed Chilies and Spices
Dried Corn Husks
Mexican Chili Supply Company
304 East Belknap
Fort Worth, Texas 76102
817-332-9896
MasterCard/Visa

Wine

Pheasant Ridge Vineyards
Rt. 3, Box 191
Lubbock, Texas 79401
806-746-6033

Llano Estacado Vineyards
P.O. Box 3487
Lubbock, Texas 79452
806-745-2258

Reservations required for large groups; small groups can stop by during business hours, Monday through Saturday, 10-4

Fall Creek Vineyards
P.O. Box 68
Tow, Texas 78672
915-379-5361

Tours and tastings are held the last Saturday of each month, 1–5 P.M.

Index